Marcel Proust Revisited

Twayne's World Authors Series
French Literature

David O'Connell, Editor

Georgia State University

TWAS 830

MARCEL PROUST

Reprinted by permission of Roger-Viollet. © Harlingue-Viollet

Marcel Proust Revisited

Barbara J. Bucknall

Brock University

Twayne Publishers • New York
Maxwell Macmillan Canada • Toronto
Maxwell Macmillan International • New York   Oxford   Singapore   Sydney

Marcel Proust Revisited
Barbara J. Bucknall

Twayne Publishers
Macmillan Publishing Company
866 Third Avenue
New York, New York 10022

Maxwell Macmillan Canada, Inc.
1200 Eglinton Avenue East
Suite 200
Don Mills, Ontario M3C 3N1

Macmillan Publishing Company is part of the Maxwell Communication Group
of Companies.

Library of Congress Cataloging-in-Publication Data

Bucknall, Barbara J.
    Marcel Proust revisited / Barbara J. Bucknall.
        p.   cm.—(Twayne's world authors series ; TWAS 830. French
    literature)
    Includes bibliographical references and index.
    ISBN 0-8057-8274-5 (alk. paper)
    1. Proust, Marcel, 1871–1922. A la recherche du temps perdu.
I. Title.   II. Series: Twayne's world authors series ; TWAS 830.
III. Series: Twayne's world authors series. French literature.
PQ2631.R63A77385   1992
843'.912—dc20   92-12879
                                                                        CIP

The paper used in this publication meets the minimum requirements
of American National Standard for Information Sciences—Permanence
of Paper for Printed Library Materials. ANSI Z3948-1984.∞™

10 9 8 7 6 5 4 3 2 1

Printed in the United States of America

Contents

Preface

Marcel Proust is known far and wide for the length and complexity of his great novel, *A la recherche du temps perdu* (*Remembrance of Things Past*), but far fewer people have read than have heard about him. Those who have read him feel like a band of initiates invited to share a special worldview, a view that takes in much that is beautiful, much that is comic, much that is charming, much that is grotesque, and much that is painful.

Proust's style is consistently beautiful, although it requires great concentration to take in a Proustian sentence. A sentence by Proust is at least as long as a paragraph in a work by his contemporary André Gide. Proust appears to be putting as much meaning, as many relationships, as many diverse and subtle points of view into a sentence as it will hold. Each sentence in *A la recherche du temps perdu* is a miniature version of the scope of the entire novel. For this reason, the metaphor has central importance for Proust because it links together aspects that might normally be considered contradictory or to have no connection. In other words, each sentence is a microcosm in the macrocosm of the entire book. Lois Marie Jaeck sees the metaphor as a microcosm and the text as macrometaphor.[1]

It may seem strange to speak in terms of a worldview to people who have not yet read Proust's great novel (since I suppose that anyone reading a guide to Proust will either not have read him or will only have read him in part). They probably know before embarking on *A la recherche du temps perdu* that Proust focuses on people who are independently wealthy and have plenty of time to go to dinner parties, read, listen to music, look at pictures, and pursue love affairs. How can such people be used to present a worldview?

Because they are human beings, and humanity is the same everywhere, in all its different guises. Each character in Proust's great novel has his or her idiosyncrasies that make him or her into a completely imagined individual. Even characters who appear relatively little, like the narrator's neighbor Legrandin, are fully alive and fully memorable, and their gyrations within the rather special society they inhabit are truer to the mechanisms of the kind of society most North Americans inhabit than might at first appear to be the case. I might mention as examples the wish to rise in society or the wish to put down people who appear to be rivals.

The aristocratic Guermantes family was idealized by the narrator in his childhood and youth because it goes so far back in time as to be touched by the magic colors of legend. It is not just their wealth and social standing that fascinate him, for he is far too much of a romantic to be impressed by money or hierarchy in a materialistic way. And that is where modern attitudes to the rich and famous part company with the attitudes Proust attributes to the social climbers in his great novel. There is something deeply poetic in many of the attitudes he describes, whereas the typical modern concern with the rich and famous is usually jealous and denigratory, like that of the Verdurins. Proust's narrator does feel disappointed when he realizes that aristocrats are only human beings, but he does not resent them for their humanity. Instead he depicts the aristocracy so truthfully that a large part of *A la recherche du temps perdu* is of genuine historical interest. In this respect, Proust himself compares it to the memoirs of Saint-Simon describing the court of Louis XIV.

Although aristocrats are very important to the narrator in one way or another, they do not compose the only class the narrator describes. The wealthy bourgeoisie also figures largely, for it is from this class that the narrator himself comes. It is represented as much more interested in the arts than the aristocracy, and, of course, its male members actually work, usually in the professions. The Verdurin circle is ridiculous in many ways, not least for its envy of the aristocracy, but M. and Mme Verdurin really are patrons of the arts; Swann, who, unlike the Verdurins, is accepted by the aristocrats, gives advice as to what paintings they should purchase; and Legrandin, who is an engineer and a social climber, is deeply involved in literature. Since the arts are very important in *A la recherche du temps perdu*, this is entirely to the credit of the bourgeoisie.

The working class is represented by prostitutes and domestic servants, including the personnel of restaurants and hotels. The chief representative is Françoise, the servant of the narrator's family. The narrator is very interested in her and her little ways, but Proust has been criticized for not taking a broader view of the working class. One great asset Françoise does have is that she is a remarkable cook. Proust's interest in the arts extends to gastronomy, although he himself became a very moderate eater, and he indicates that Françoise deserves respect, if only for her culinary feats.

Connecting these different and separate classes is the theme of sex, particularly homosexuality. As the book continues, homosexuality acquires increasing importance until it comes to seem that the heterosexuals are actually in the minority. Being homosexual himself, Proust took a natural interest in the subject, but his homosexuals are not idealized in the least. Most of the time they seem grotesque and comic, a method of portraiture that made his reading public able to accept the explicitness of his descriptions. At other times they are tragic figures and evoke pity. As a result, Proust may have done as much to create an atmosphere of tolerance for homosexuals as did André Gide with his more direct approach, although few modern "gays" would appreciate a tolerance based on laughter and pity.

The narrator is an observer of all these aspects of society, but he is happiest in the bosom of his family, particularly with his mother and grandmother. He is also happy gazing at the beauties of nature: there are many ravishing descriptions of flowers and the sea in this novel. He admired the paintings of the impressionists, but his own flower paintings very detailed, like those of Dutch old masters. He responds intensely to beauty, and as Philip Kolb says, he is guided on his way by four "beacons."[2] This is a reference to Baudelaire's poem "Les Phares," which celebrates great artists. Proust's fictional four "beacons" are Berma, the great actress, Bergotte, the great writer, Elstir, the great artist, and Vinteuil, the great composer. Inspired by their example the narrator finally rises above mundane things and becomes a great writer himself. Their position in the society Proust depicts is irrelevant because they belong to a completely different and far superior domain. Their works belong to eternity and not to time.

Time is the last word on the narrator's lips when the novel ends. Countless critics have commented on the importance of time and memory in Proust's work, adding as it does a fourth dimension. It was to give an adequate impression of the passage of time that Proust made his novel so long and so full of changes. This alone would have made Proust remarkable without all the other riches he bestows on his readers.

Finally, I will say that I have attempted to do justice to all these important aspects of *A la recherche du temps perdu*, but that, since time affects readers as well as writers, I have a different view of this novel than I did when I first started to study Proust. Since I love beauty myself, the beauty of Proust's great novel affected me very deeply on first reading. On this most recent rereading I have experienced it, as do most modern readers, as what the Germans call a bildungsroman,[3] that is, a novel that takes the protagonist from immaturity to maturity, and it is on this interpretation that I have mainly concentrated my efforts.

I should also explain my choice of edition. Because a great deal of previously unpublished material pertaining to *A la recherche du temps perdu* has been made available for study since the publication of the first scholarly edition by Pierre Clarac and André Ferré for Gallimard (Pléiade) in 1954, three new editions of *A la recherche du temps perdu* have come on the market. The new Gallimard edition by Jean-Yves Tadié is the most scholarly, and the one published by Robert Laffont is the least scholarly. I have based my guide to Proust's great novel on an intermediate edition, published by Flammarion and edited by Jean Milly. For *Contre Sainte-Beuve* (*Against Sainte-Beuve*) I have used the Pléiade edition edited by Pierre Clarac and Yves Sandré. For *Les Plaisirs et les jours* (*Pleasures and Regrets*) and *Jean Santeuil* I have used the Pléiade edition with the same editors.

I have not used many quotations. I have preferred to paraphrase, partly because I want this guide to Proust to be as readable as possible and partly because I would like it to be useful to people using any of the editions, including the English translations. Where the editions differ, I have tried to point these differences out without being pedantic.

Finally, I should add that 30 years have elapsed since I started reading Proust and Proust criticism, and I may have inadvertently absorbed some Proust criticism to the point where I reproduce it without realizing where I got these ideas in the first place. I have tried to acknowledge borrowings whenever I may have been able to identify them, but the main body of this text represents how I, personally, read Proust at the present moment.

Acknowledgments

I wish to thank the firm of Roger-Viollet for permission to use a photograph of Marcel Proust for this book.

I also wish to thank Philip Kolb for his unfailing support and encouragement over the years. Moreover, I wish to acknowledge my debts to Henry Bonnet, who welcomed me to the Société des Amis de Marcel Proust, and to Charles Whiting, my doctoral dissertation director, for their support and encouragement.

Chronology

1871   Born 10 July in Auteuil.

1881   Has his first attack of asthma.

1888   Begins to publish articles and vignettes.

1889   Meets Anatole France and his hostess, Mme Arman de Caillavet. Begins his one-year military service.

1892   Starts *Le Banquet* with the help of some friends.

1893   Introduced to Comte Robert de Montesquiou and Comtesse Greffulhe. Receives his degree in law.

1895   Receives his degree in philosophy. Accepts position at the Bibliothèque Mazarine, but immediately takes leave of absence. Begins *Jean Santeuil*.

1896   *Les Plaisirs et les jours.*

1897   Fights a duel with Jean Lorrain over insinuations about his relationship with Lucien Daudet.

1898   Dreyfus affair begins; supports Dreyfus.

1903   Father dies.

1904   *La Bible d'Amiens*, translated from Ruskin's *Bible of Amiens*.

1905   Mother dies; emotionally devastated, he goes into a clinic.

1906   *Sésame et les lys*, translated from Ruskin's *Sesame and Lilies*.

1907   Befriends Alfred Agostinelli.

1908   *Pastiches* on Lemoine affair. Works on *Contre Sainte-Beuve*. Agostinelli enters his service.

1909   Begins *A la recherche du temps perdu*. Attempts to publish *Contre Sainte-Beuve*, without success.

1912   Approaches publishers for his novel without success.

1913   *Du côté de chez Swann* is published by Grasset at the author's expense. Céleste Albaret enters his service. Agostinelli leaves to become an aviator.

1914   Agostinelli dies in a flying accident. Grasset closes because of the war.

1916   Invited by André Gide, who had previously refused him, to accept publication with the *Nouvelle Revue Française* (Gallimard).

1919   *Du côté de chez Swann, A l'ombre des jeunes filles en fleurs, Pastiches et mélanges.* Wins the Goncourt Prize for *A l'ombre des jeunes filles en fleurs.*

1920   Awarded the Legion of Honor. *Le Côté de Guermantes 1.*

1921   *Le Côté de Guermantes 2; Sodome et Gomorrhe 1.*

1922   *Sodome et Gomorrhe 2; Sodome et Gomorrhe 3; La Prisonnière.* Dies 18 November.

1925   *Albertine disparue.*

1927   *Le Temps retrouvé. Chroniques.*

1952   *Jean Santeuil*, ed. Bernard de Fallois.

1954   *Contre Sainte-Beuve* with *Nouveaux mélanges*, ed. Bernard de Fallois.

Chapter One
Proust's Life and Works

Marcel Proust was born in Auteuil on 10 July 1871, the son of Dr. Adrien Proust and Mme Proust, née Jeanne Weil. His father was an eminent and greatly respected physician; his mother, who was Jewish, was beautiful, sensitive, and highly cultured. Two years later, they had another son, Robert, but Marcel was always his mother's favorite. They lived in Paris but spent their Easter and summer vacations in the little town of Illiers, Dr. Proust's hometown. In honor of Proust, it is now called Illiers-Combray, Combray being the name Proust gave to the fictional small town where the narrator of *A la recherche du temps perdu* spends his vacations.

Proust first became aware that he was homosexual in high school.[1] (Proust disliked the word "homosexual," but the word he preferred, "invert," is considered insulting nowadays. My use of the word "gay" would be anachronistic.) The opprobrium attached to homosexuality naturally disturbed him personally, and he was deeply distressed to think of the pain his sexual orientation would give his mother if she found out. He was only too aware of his parents' disappointment in him because of his reluctance to embark on a proper career. His brother, Robert, became a doctor like his father, but Marcel knew that writing would be the only career that would suit him. He had the income to pursue this vocation, but his parents considered his ambition frivolous. The nearest he came to doing any "serious" work was to accept employment with the Bibliothèque Mazarine (in 1895), but he remained on leave until he was dismissed. He began his leave by taking a trip to Brittany with his friend and lover, Reynaldo Hahn, a gifted composer and musician.

Even had he not wanted to become a writer, ill health would probably have prevented him from taking up a more conventional career. He had been subject to asthma since the age of nine, and he was convinced that if he stayed up all night and slept by day his asthma attacks would be less intense. Moreover his nerves were not in good shape. He was extremely sensitive and easily hurt; he supposed that nobody loved him except his mother and grandmother; and he spent a great deal of time and effort trying to buy love with compliments and money.

He had a brilliant mind and was a gifted writer from childhood. He also loved to read, an occupation that stimulated his desire and ability to write. Although his school compositions were brilliant and original, it took him a very long time to find his own voice. Like the narrator in "Combray," he had such an idealized notion of literature that when he tried to think of a topic sufficiently exalted for him to write about, his mind went blank. But the fact that he and his mother constantly wrote little notes to each other shows that Proust preferred to express his deepest and tenderest feelings in writing rather than through face-to-face conversation. The same might be said of the other letters he wrote. Philip Kolb's edition of Proust's letters so far covers 1880 to 1920, and runs to 19 volumes. Proust was such a voluminous letter writer because he felt more at ease setting down his thoughts and feelings on paper. He could concentrate on them without any interruptions or distractions from an interlocutor. He could express exactly what he felt in the aptest terms. Writing helped him to control the situation, whatever it was, as one solitude impinging on another and making an impression at a very deep level. Moreover, as his health deteriorated, writing letters became absolutely necessary to keep in touch with his friends, his editor, and his publisher.

However, his letters, although they were so remarkable that their recipients saved them, took up time and energy that he felt would have been better employed for works of literature, as the narrator comes to realize at the end of *Le Temps retrouvé*. But they do provide us with a great deal of valuable information about his life and works.

He broke into print quite young, with his first book, *Les Plaisirs et les jours* (*Pleasure and Regrets*), published in 1896, at a stage in his life when he was very active socially. This book is not at all profound. Parts of it acknowledge the virtues of solitude, which shows that Proust himself was aware of the mistake he was making. But he was chagrined when his friends laughed at his book, and particularly at the adventitious aids Proust had used to enhance it, namely, a preface by Anatole France and illustrations by Madeleine Lemaire. *Les Plaisirs et les jours* is peopled with aristocrats with very fanciful names, and at least some of the stories, such as "La Mort de Baldassare Silvande," seem to suggest that what would be uninteresting in a plebeian or bourgeois setting immediately has the power to fascinate when performed by an aristocrat.

At the same time, *Les Plaisirs et les jours* indicates that a taste for society life is a grave spiritual danger; this same idea will be developed more fully in *A la recherche du temps perdu*. The danger society poses is portrayed in a particularly striking way in "Violante ou la mondanité," in which Proust suggest that a life of solitary retirement is the only way to achieve health and happiness. Society is also represented as a danger in "La Confession d'une jeune fille," but here sex too is a threat. The "jeune fille" in question is deeply ashamed of her sex life, tries to suppress her sexual desires by becoming active in high society, but then reverts to sex again. Her mother catches her engaged in a sexual act and dies of shock. The "jeune fille" then commits suicide. This tale obviously reflects Proust's guilty fears of how his own mother would react to discovering his homosexuality. "La Confession d'une jeune fille" is interesting as Proust's first attempt to discuss the subject. This will not be the last time he would attribute his own sexual guilt to a fictional feminine stand-in.

This statement may seem opaque to those readers who come to Proust for the first time. In *A la recherche du temps perdu* Proust's narrator shows tolerance for homosexuals but animosity for lesbians. Proust's greatest love was Alfred Agostinelli. Proust was apparently jealous of his young friend's mistress. When he wrote his great novel he combined some of the characteristics of Agostinelli with some of the features of Agostinelli's relationship with his mistress to produce the narrator's great love, Albertine, a lesbian.

Proust, who was only 25 when *Les Plaisirs et les jours* was published, showed little promise of exceptional achievement. The miracle of the transformation of the mundane into the substance of true art had not taken place nor would it for some time to come. *Jean Santeuil*, which Proust started in 1895, shows no advance on the previous work, apart from the fact that it is much less precious. Unfortunately, this does not necessarily mean that it is better: most of *Jean Santeuil* is simply dull. Proust was apparently trying to avoid using the purple prose to which his teacher Alphonse Darlu (here portrayed under the name of M. Beulier) had objected. This novel remained fragmentary and was not published until Bernard de Fallois's edited text appeared in 1952.

Jean Santeuil has interest because it allows us to see Proust handling many topics that appear in *A la recherche de temps perdu*, and to marvel at the difference between apprentice work and master work. *Jean Santeuil* is in many ways a step backward from *Les Plaisirs et les jours*. The pleasure of associating with aristocrats is presented without any criticism, and Proust even goes so far as to let us know that for his hero to be seen by an enemy while taking a stroll with a duchess is the height of glory. The conversation of the characters is extremely uninteresting, in contrast to the skill with which Proust handles conversation in *A la recherche du temps perdu*. In contrast to Proust's earlier attempt to grapple with the problems of homosexuals, here he tries to discuss them, as Milton Hindus has pointed out,[2] in terms of a politician's embezzlement of public funds. This is very far from the subject.

Certain episodes are interesting, however, if only because Proust is making use of actual persons or events. The Dreyfus affair puts in an appearance. So does Mme de Noailles, the gifted poet. Jaurès comes on the scene to make a political statement. But the most striking example of real life appearing untransformed and in the raw comes when Jean breaks a Venetian-glass vase because he is angry with his parents, and his mother says that this act will be the symbol of their indestructible union, as in a Jewish marriage. A mother like that is hard to shake off, particularly when you enjoy her company.

Around the time that he was writing *Jean Santeuil*, Proust took a passionate interest in the Dreyfus affair. Dreyfus was a Jewish captain in the French army who was convicted of selling military secrets to the Germans and imprisoned on Devil's Island. In actual fact he was innocent, but the army did not wish to admit its mistake. Thirteen years passed before he was rehabilitated. The Dreyfus case figures largely in *Le Côté de Guermantes*, where Proust shows how France was divided on the subject. Proust himself did what he could to alert the public to Dreyfus's innocence, but in the narrator in *Le Côté de Guermantes* is much more detached. This is one of the many ways in which Proust is similar to but different from the narrator.

In 1897 Proust discovered the English writer Ruskin and proceeded to study him and write articles about him. Eventually he translated Ruskin's *The Bible of Amiens* and *Sesame and Lilies*, published respectively in 1904 and 1906.

What Ruskin had to say about French church architecture fascinated Proust so much that in 1907 he visited several French cathedrals, trying to see them through the eyes of Ruskin. He also made use of the works of Emile Mâle, a specialist in gothic architecture. What he wrote about Ruskin was a real improvement on what he had written before; his preface to *Sésame et les lys* is as good as anything in "Combray," which it prefigures. In the preface of *La Bible d'Amiens* he speaks of Ruskin in terms of biblical hyperbole to show his intense respect for the great English author. Normally, when Proust heaps compliments on someone's head, the effect is a little suspect, but here Proust's admiration seems genuine, if a little overornamented.

There is such an astonishing difference between *Les Plaisirs et les jours* and *Jean Santeuil*, on the one hand, and *A la recherche du temps perdu*, on the other, that it makes one wonder what miracle could have caused it. Proust's developing skills were in part due to sheer perseverance, but it also seems true that his immersion in Ruskin took Proust out of himself and encouraged him to work to the utmost of his power.

Another change came about around this time, one that cannot be attributed to the influence of Ruskin. Proust started to reveal his sense of humor. It was not that he had been incapable of humor earlier: the pretensions of Comte Robert de Montesquiou, who was to serve as the model for the character Baron de Charlus, often sent him into gales of helpless laughter. But during his writing apprenticeship he seems to have felt that "serious" literature should not be funny. There is one comic interlude in *Les Plaisirs et les jours*, "Mondanité et mélomanie de Bouvard et Pécuchet," but there is very little that is amusing about *Jean Santeuil*. The discovery of humor first became apparent in the *pastiches* (articles written in the style of various famous authors) which he started publishing in *Le Figaro* in 1908. (These were all published together in his *Pastiches et mélanges* in 1919.)

It is puzzling that this change took place after his mother's death in 1905. He missed his mother very much and even had to seek refuge in a sanatorium to recover from his loss. Perhaps he felt more at liberty to write what he chose without her looking over his shoulder. He could be himself more easily if he did not have to refer everything back to this beloved judge. Moreover, Proust's sense of humor, as we will see in *Le Côté de Guermantes*, was not far removed from a sense of the tragic, for it is very much based on the grotesque and the absurd.

Certainly it would be outrageous to suggest that he forgot his mother. The trip with her to Venice and Padua in 1900 inspired part of *La Fugitive*, in which the narrator's mother is closely based on Mme Proust, and she became his imagined companion in *Contre Sainte-Beuve*, written in 1908 and 1909 (but not published until 1954). In this work Proust attacks Sainte-Beuve's conviction that a good critic should take cognizance of an author's life as well as of his works, and practices his own, intuitive method on some of his favorite writers, specifically Gérard de Nerval, Baudelaire, Balzac, and Flaubert, whom Sainte-Beuve did not appreciate sufficiently. By this time *A la recherche du temps perdu* was taking shape in his mind.

Someone who would have a very important part to play in this work was Alfred Agostinelli, who drove Proust through Normandy in the summer of 1907. Proust deeply loved Agostinelli, whom he made his secretary in 1913 in order to keep him close at hand, but he was not successful in damping the young man's love of adventure, and Agostinelli soon decided to become an aviator. He died as the result of a flying accident near Antibes in 1914. He served as the model for Albertine; indeed, Proust used their actual letters in *La Fugitive* for the letters between the narrator and Albertine. Before Agostinelli had his accident, Proust sent an emissary to bring him back, just as the narrator of *A la recherche du temps perdu* sends Robert de Saint-Loup to bring Albertine back from Touraine.

We have already noticed that Proust incorporated people and places he knew in his great novel. He acknowledged that he had little imagination, in the sense that he could not make things up out of whole cloth. But he did transform the things he took from real life, often blending together in the delineation of a character traits he took from several different people. There is not space to go into this practice in any detail here; for this kind of interpretation I highly recommend George D. Painter's *Marcel Proust: A Biography*.

In 1909 Proust decided to spend as much time as possible writing and as little time as possible socializing. As he wrote to Mme Straus, he immediately roughed out the beginning and the end of his great book.[3] (Antoine Compagnon has expressed doubts about this claim).[4] Proust had difficulty finding a publisher for *Du côté de chez Swann* and finally had to publish it at his own expense through the publisher Grasset in 1913. Proust was unable to continue publication during World War I, and during those war years Proust expanded his novel considerably. *Du côté de chez Swann* met with a lukewarm critical reception, but *A l'ombre des jeunes filles en fleurs,* which appeared in 1919, was awarded the Goncourt Prize. Proust had already switched from Grasset to the more prestigious house of Gallimard, where he no longer had to publish at his own expense.

Le Côté de Guermantes, part 1, was published in 1920. *Le Côté de Guermantes*, part 2, was published together with *Sodome et Gomorrhe*, part 1, in 1921. *Sodome et Gomorrhe*, parts 2 and 3, and *La Prisonnière* were published in 1922, the year of Proust's death. Even his own death contributed to his great novel, since he used his own experience of severe illness as a basis for the death of Bergotte, his example of a great writer. Reciprocally, his great novel contributed to his death, because he refused to stop writing when he was dying of pneumonia. Céleste Albaret, who had entered Proust's service in 1913, was with him to the last, having devoted herself to him entirely. Her presence must have been a comfort to him. His doctor brother, Robert, also tried to save him.

La Fugitive under the title *Albertine disparue* appeared in 1925, and *Le Temps retrouvé* appeared in 1927. Since Proust could not supervise their publication, these volumes are marred by inconsistencies and incoherences, as is *La Prisonnière* but the total effect of each volume is so striking that one hardly notices their flaws. Proust had achieved his aim of being a great writer at the cost of his life. His dedication to his vocation is unparalleled in the domain of literature.

Chapter Two
Du côté de chez Swann (Swann's Way)

Part 1 "Combray," chapter 1

Proust starts his enormous novel by having the narrator state that for a long time he went to bed early and that as he dropped off to sleep he would imagine that he was the subject of the book he was reading. This is not the kind of opening guaranteed to grip the average reader and make him want to read on. But Proust, like other great writers of his time, such as Mallarmé and Joyce, envisioned the act of reading his book as a kind of quest, which the reader could only achieve though dedication, perseverance, imagination, and effort. The opening section of the first volume tantalizes the reader with all kinds of vague suggestions about the notions that enter the narrator's mind as he lies in bed. Times and places and people are all mixed up together. Most of the places and people the reader first hears about will not be identified and explained until much further on. Proust speaks of a kaleidoscope, the kaleidoscope of darkness, and there is a truly kaleidoscopic effect here.

Scott Moncrieff, in his translation *Remembrance of Things Past*, groups together the opening sections under the heading "The Overture." Indeed, the whole of *Du côté de chez Swann* is a kind of overture. Certain themes, with variations, are repeated again and again, while other themes are introduced and then dropped, only to be reintroduced at a much later time, so that we suppose that Proust had completely changed the subject. His method of organization is so hidden in the early sections that many of his early critics thought he was just rambling on in a process of free association.

Robert Vigneron has speculated that Proust's early death was a merciful release for his readers, because nothing else could have made him stop adding to his book in one way or another.[1] In fact, the manner in which Proust begins his great novel indicates that there is no particular point at which he need end, because the opening pages are actually situated, in terms of the narrator's life, somewhere in the middle. It is true that in the first volume he then goes on to talk of his childhood, while in the last volume, *Le Temps retrouvé*, the narrator expresses fear that his death is near. But the narrator's imminent death is not the true end of the book, since the real conclusion is his decision to write the novel we have just read. Thus the narrative is circular, not linear.

Some of the main themes around which Proust constructs his novel, themes that he will continually take up and elaborate on indefinitely, appear in these opening pages. These main themes include time, memory, dreams, and illusion. In their grip, the narrator is subject to error, but he struggles to find truth, alone and unaided. He is in the dark in more ways than one. And despite flashes of perceptive insight, this will be the narrator's situation throughout most of his existence.

It is possible to view *A la Recherche du temps perdu* as a detective novel not unlike Alain Robbe-Grillet's *Les Gommes (The Erasers)*[2] in that, although the detective pursues various suspects, he turns out to be himself the wanted man. The narrator searches endlessly for truth, but the truth that he is finally vouchsafed is the truth of his own life and his own being. In this search time is short but the narrator behaves as if time were endless. The opening pages, which at first sight may seem confusing and irrelevant, introduce the real subject, which is not a particular, individual life, but the fundamental dilemma of mankind. "Know thyself" was probably an old maxim even at the time of the ancient Greeks, but the passage of time had made it no easier to put into practice. Proust shows us how one man might learn to know himself, and thus how we might too, sooner or later. Thus ignorance, error, truth, and self-knowledge can be added to our list of introductory themes.

From bewilderment and confusion, the narrator moves on to something that is absolutely clear to him, the childhood agony he went through over his desire for his mother's goodnight kiss. In a curious way, as Raymond T. Riva points out, Proust parallels Freud,[3] even though he never read him. However, for Proust, the traumatic childhood incidents are easily remembered, while the happy ones are sunk in oblivion and have to be recalled for the sake of mental health. Now the memory of one unhappy night in particular is so present to the narrator that he mulls it over repeatedly. For the time being, all the rest of his childhood is obliterated by this particular memory.

Proust is like Freud because both begin the search for self-knowledge by going back to childhood. Extraordinary self-knowledge is revealed in this evocation of childhood, as Proust mingles laughter and tears in his portrayal of the tragic absurdity of the narrator's longing for his mother's goodnight kiss and his desperate attempts to get it. Proust, through his narrator, also reveals a great deal of knowledge of other people, to which the child's unusually perceptive and mature comments on the adults around him bear witness. This child is so knowing that he seems too old to need his mother's kiss (many of Proust's readers have wondered how old he actually is).

It may, of course, be possible to say that the child is old before his time, perhaps because so many of his relatives are old. The family gathered around the dinner table in the garden of Aunt Léonie's house in Combray consists of the narrator as child, his father and mother, his grandfather and grandmother, and his grandmother's two sisters and another great-aunt. The conversation, when this group is joined by their friend M. Swann, is well above any normal child's head. But he takes it all in, although he claims to be indifferent to everything but his mother's kiss.

Is this an oedipal situation? Were Proust aware of the Oedipus complex, he might possibly reply that it is not, because the adult narrator, commenting on the child he was, implies that this kind of anxiety about being separated from the person one loves (that is, when the child goes to bed) is a kind of preparation for adult love and can be transferred to it, but it is not the same thing. It must be admitted, however, that this episode certainly has striking oedipal parallels: the child narrator manages to get his mother away from his father for the night, he is overcome by guilt at what he has done, and then, to cheer him up, his mother reads him a love story—*François le Champi* (François the foundling) by George Sand—while, however, omitting all the love passages. Things are like adult love and yet are not. Perhaps Freud's theory of childhood is not all that dissimilar to Proust's portrait.

Proust had cunningly used the theme of memory to make a transition to the theme of love, which will be central throughout his novel and which will be indelibly imprinted with the stamp of suffering, separation, and possessive jealousy. The narrator already notes in this episode that Swann would have understood how he felt, and three episodes later Proust tells us why Swann would understand the child's feelings. It was Proust's own belief, and not merely an opinion attributed to the narrator, that love is accompanied by anguish; love not accompanied by anguish is not true love.

However, I am giving a false impression of this episode by suggesting that the narrator's mother is of central importance. Almost equally important is the narrator's grandmother, who is laughed at and tormented by certain other members of the family because of her love of nature and beauty. She wishes the narrator to be brought up to love whatever is noble and beautiful. She is extremely altruistic and thinks nothing of putting her own health at risk to make her little grandson happy. She introduces him to works of art, including the pastoral novels of George Sand, from which his mother selects *François le Champi*. When the narrator dedicates himself to writing later on, it is largely due to her—even if her love of the beautiful leads her to purchase decorative chairs that collapse when the recipient attempts to sit on one, much to the amusement of her family.

From the episode of the goodnight kiss, which Proustians call *le drame du coucher* (the bedtime drama),[4] Proust moves on to the most famous episode in his great novel, the episode of the madeleine. A doctor once informed me that he had studied this part of the text in Harvard Medical School as an example of the way in which certain gustatory, tactile, and olfactory sensations can bring back very vivid memories of previous scenes and events—so vivid, that they actually seem to be present. Here is another example, if one were needed, of Proust's acuteness as a psychologist.

In this episode memory triumphs over time and oblivion and brings back all the narrator's happy memories of his childhood. But the memory at work here is what Proust calls *involuntary memory*, not the ordinary kind of memory. Involuntary memory will continue to have enormous importance throughout the novel; indeed, it will conclude with a whole series of involuntary memories in the last volume. But for a long time the reader is left with the impression that the episode of the madeleine is the only example of the power of involuntary memory in the book. Proust expects his readers to have very good memories—of the ordinary kind.

The madeleine in question is an ordinary French teacake, with a flavor something like pound cake, only lighter and crisper. The madeleine is primarily notable for its unusual shape, which is that of a scallop shell. As I heard Philip Kolb point out, the shape carries religious overtones, for the scallop shell is the symbol of Saint James the Apostle. But shape alone is not responsible for the tones of awe in which the narrator speaks of the effect it has on him. Taste too is important. He dunks it in some lindenflower tea—a drink which itself is quite insipid—and as he tastes it, he feels an overwhelming bliss. He struggles to identify the source of this joy, and then his childhood days in Combray return to overwhelm him.

The whole episode is so magical that many people suppose that there is something intrinsically wonderful about the taste of a madeleine dunked in lindenflower tea. In actual fact, this phenomenon depends entirely on encountering a taste or smell that one has not encountered for a long time, one that carries with it strong emotional associations. Porridge or bagels would work just as well as madeleines if the right conditions were met. But you cannot make involuntary memory happen. It can only happen spontaneously. Hence the narrator's feeling of experiencing something miraculous.

The moral of this, it seems to me, is that, however wise or acute Proust's psychological insights may be, one should always bear in mind that, just as the narrator is on a quest for self-knowledge, *A la recherche du temps perdu* cannot be treated as a substitute for one's own quest. It can be very valuable as an incitement or even a guide in one own's quest for self-knowledge, but Proust's truths are not always our truths, nor would he have wished them to be. The kaleidoscope turns, in the hands of each reader, and the same elements form different patterns.

Part 1 "Combray," chapter 2

Now we come to the complete evocation of Combray, the little town where the narrator and his family spent their vacations, in the home of the narrator's great-aunt and her daughter, Aunt Léonie. Aunt Léonie was not described in the *drame du coucher* because she is an invalid and therefore was not present at the family gathering. She is closely associated with the madeleine episode, however, for it was she who in the past used to give the narrator a piece of madeleine dunked in lindenflower tea.

It is impossible to dart from subject to subject as the narrator does in this part of the book without giving the impression of meandering at random from reminiscence to reminiscence. But in actual fact the whole thing forms a tightly woven fabric once the reader enters deep enough into the text to recognize Proust's methods and themes. I will make an exception to my usual practice throughout this analysis of staying close to the narrative, and here follow certain themes as they occur throughout the depiction of Combray. I start with Aunt Léonie, because Proust starts with her.

When we meet Aunt Léonie, we realize that the narrator, who is such an odd little boy himself, is fascinated by oddness in other people, to the point of being the more fond of people the more eccentric they are. We can call this theme "the theme of the bizarre." It will reach amazing heights later in the narrator's depiction of homosexual men and women, but for the time being Proust carefully limits himself to such traits as Aunt Léonie as her dubious but imperious claim to be incapable of sleep, and her insistence that people consider her genuinely ill and at the same time certain to live forever.

In a tone of amusement that expresses real love, the narrator describes his aunt's pleasure at eating off plates painted with themes from the *Arabian Nights*, her frustration when the parish priest suggests that she climb the church tower, her endless curiosity about her neighbors, and her use of the maid, Françoise, as a source of information. Françoise and a constant visitor, Eulalie, are her only sources of information outside the family, and she ends up creating a paranoid and sadomasochistic drama in which she suspects each of them in turn of plotting behind her back. Her paranoia does not change the narrator's attitude toward her. And she is equally fond of him: when she dies she leaves him her entire fortune.

Françoise appears to be the perfect servant, so devoted to Aunt Léonie that she still loves her in spite of—or because of—the way Aunt Léonie treats her. Perhaps they are kindred spirits, for Françoise can be even more cruel than her employer. The narrator is shocked to hear Françoise, while killing a chicken, exclaim "Sale bête" (Filthy beast) but he does not seem particularly distressed by her reluctance to help the kitchen maid when she becomes sick following labor, by the sarcasms she utters when she does come to the kitchen maid's aid, or even by his belated discovery that Françoise constantly fed the family asparagus because it gave the kitchen maid asthma. There is a good deal of cruelty mixed up with Proust's humor, even though he objected to cruelty on principle. But perhaps he wanted to expose the narrator as someone less nice than he thinks himself to be. Cruelty and suffering are certainly dominant themes in *A la recherche du temps perdu*; both are frequently combined with absurdity.

When it comes to the bizarre combined with total absurdity, it is hard to know whether to award the prize to the narrator's school friend Bloch or to the adult Legrandin, who takes a surprising interest in the youthful narrator. Bloch talks about literature in a very bizarre way, combining high-flown literary language with vulgar slang. The narrator seems fascinated by his conversation and accepts him as a guide, but Bloch is eventually forbidden the narrator's house after he slanders the great-aunt. Apparently he does not care what he says, so long as he can say it in a really striking way. In addition, he is a Jew, and the narrator's family is ever so slightly anti-Semitic. Perhaps Proust, who was Jewish himself on his mother's side, was engaged in a little self-torture when he created

Bloch, and coped with his anguish by making anti-Semitism sound funny. Maurice Samuel has suggested that the narrator was actually a Jew himself and did not want us to know it, but that is only one possible reading.[5]

Legrandin's style of conversation is bizarre too, in his case because it is so exclusively literary. He talks, quite literally, like a book. His absurdity consists of the social climbing he attempts to, but cannot, conceal from the precocious boy and his family, even though he makes the most frantic efforts to do so. He is probably already homosexual (he is not revealed to be homosexual until much later in the story) and, as is the case with homosexuals throughout this novel, his sexual identity partially accounts for his bizarre style and conduct, which are motivated by the wish to conceal something that is glaringly obvious, once the right key has been found. Social climbing and homosexuality will be very important themes in *A la recherche du temps perdu*.

Another bizarre person who attracts the narrator, so much so that he wants to kiss her, is Mlle Vinteuil, the daughter of the local piano teacher, who is a brilliant but unknown composer. Her appearance and manner are those of a boy and a girl at the same time, and she grows up to be a lesbian. The narrator, who appears to be in his teens in this episode, catches sight of her and her lover through the window of Montjouvain, the house M. Vinteuil left to his daughter. Comments made about their activities appear to be those of the adult narrator rather than the teenage one, yet we are left with the impression that the narrator feels sympathy and understanding, even when Mlle Vinteuil encourages her lover to spit on her father's portrait, a piece of behavior which the narrator considers sadistic, but which he excuses, on the grounds that Mlle Vinteuil is so virtuous that she has to perform acts that she believes to be evil in order to be capable of erotic enjoyment. He considers this typical of the sadist, of whom he has an immediate understanding. The narrator's later attitude to lesbians will be very different.

Although the narrator depicts himself as a judge of others most of the time, there are moments in "Combray," as in other parts of *A la recherche du temps perdu*, where he attributes bizarre and comical behavior to himself. This self-dissection was already apparent in *le drame du coucher*. It is also apparent in this part of "Combray," for instance, when the boy rushes off, while in Paris, to visit his Uncle Adolphe's house, hoping to surprise him with an actress, since he is so desperately eager to meet actresses, and does in fact find his uncle with a courtesan. (The actress was not very different from a courtesan in those days.) She is "la dame en rose" (the lady in pink) who is later identified with Mme Swann. This visit is a source of great embarrassment for Uncle Adolphe and of indignation for the narrator's family.

In this episode the narrator from his older point of view has a good laugh at his own youthful naïveté, as he does again when his child self comes face to face with the little Gilberte Swann while taking a walk past Swann's estate, and believes that she is insulting him when she is actually making a gesture of sexual invitation. His immediate response is to want to tell her that she is ugly and repulsive, in order to make some kind of impression on her. His reaction is so inappropriate to the actual facts of the case that he appears ridiculous to both narrator and reader. Throughout the book, the narrator will frequently invite us to laugh *at* him as well as *with* him. Although he is very perceptive at certain moments, he can be quite blind at other times. The reader's task is to distinguish when he is really blind at those moments when he would like to persuade us that he is being perceptive. Self-knowledge is a long process, arrived at by realizing error after error.

One area in which the narrator makes relatively few mistakes, although even here he does make some, is in the realm of the aesthetic. As a child, he has a very strong, instinctive reaction to beauty, whether in nature, architecture, or literature. He is less responsive, for the time being, to painting, and music is not mentioned in "Combray," because M. Vinteuil is too shy to play his compositions to his visitors. But in his adult life he will have an overwhelming response to painting and music.

The parish church of Combray is the first repository of the beautiful to be described. In truth, the parish church of Illiers, the country town where Proust spent his childhood vacations, is quite ugly. Much of what Proust had to say about the parish church of Combray is based on other churches and cathedrals, as Luc Fraisse points out,[6] particularly on the cathedral at Chartres, which is famous for its stained glass. In fact, it is chiefly the stained-glass windows of the parish church that excite the narrator when he describes it, in prose of the utmost magnificence. These stained-glass windows, with their ever-changing light effects, cast an enchantment over the whole church. The narrator also celebrates the church's many historical treasures. Proust leaves us in no doubt that the church is a magical place, partly because of its beauty and partly because it has survived so successfully through many centuries of time, its fourth dimension. That it is sacred from the religious point of view, Proust does not deny. He even compares its steeple to the finger of God. But he mixes a great many magical associations in with the few religious ones, and he leaves us in no doubt that it is the former that really count for the boy. By combining the beautiful with the supernatural, he is beginning to concoct his own religion of beauty.

The next focus of artistic merit to appear is a collection of photographs of Giotto's Virtues and Vices from the Chapel of the Arena in Padua. The boy does not really appreciate their symbolic value and blames them for not being sufficiently sentimental and "realistic," but later on he will come to appreciate the special kind of truth and beauty they convey. He mentions that it was M. Swann who gave him these photographs—M. Swann will later mediate his approach to literature.

Of all the creative arts, literature is the one that most holds the youthful narrator spellbound, and with good reason. He has a curious problem: he finds it very difficult to enter directly into contact with reality. The narrator, with his strange ability to enter into other people's minds, *contains* people rather than *sees* them, and he can contain the characters in books even more completely than people from real life. In fact, he can contain whole lifetimes, which pass too slowly in reality to be perceptible. When he spends Sunday afternoons reading, he is absorbing a spiritual nourishment that is essential to him, because it makes him feel, for once, in complete contact.

Dreams of love, only one step removed from the masturbation in which he engages, are increasingly associated with his reading, and for the same reason. There is no way he can get into contact with a real girl or woman, and neither his mother nor his grandmother nor Aunt Léonie would do as the object of his romantic dreams. He builds an imaginary bridge between himself and Gilberte Swann when M. Swann tells the narrator that Bergotte is a family friend. Bergotte, partly based on Anatole France, is Proust's invented example of the truly great writer. But this imaginary bridge does nothing to help the narrator to establish contact with Gilberte when he finally sees her. A great lady, the Duchesse de Guermantes, is also associated romantically with his reading (and with the slides of his magic lantern and the treasures of the parish church), but when he sees her, he reacts by conceiving a fervent admiration for the aristocracy that does not lead him any closer to true love. In fact, for the rest of the book his romantic dreams, based on literature, will never give him satisfaction even when they come true.

However, the narrator does have a very great compensation for his failures in love. Like W. B. Yeats and Thomas Mann, Proust believed that one could not be perfect both in one's life and in one's work.[7] The narrator is destined to become a great writer, although he wastes a great deal of time on foolish notions about how he is to accomplish this destiny. However, the episode of the steeples of Martinville, in which the narrator writes down what he actually feels about them, gives him such happiness that this act and its emotional consequences provide him with sufficient indication that he is doing the right thing. It is an axiom of Proust's that, however much a creative artist may suffer in his life, his creative activity brings him joy.

The steeples of Martinville form part of a landscape. We learn that viewing natural beauty gives the narrator as much joy as reading. He is particularly susceptible to flowers, which he associates with girls. When he views the sprays of hawthorn set on the altar for the Month of Mary, he does so with mixed erotic and religious emotions. The same emotion will affect him even more strongly when he sees the pink hawthorn in Swann's park, just before seeing Gilberte, the color of whose hair is almost pink. Flowers are beautiful, erotic, and religious. Flowers as well as other natural objects will accompany the budding writer on his long pilgrimage to true creativity. In fact this episode ends with a tribute to the two country "ways" or paths along which the narrator and his family used to take their afternoon walks—Swann's way, after which this volume is named, and the Guermantes way—and which have left an indelible impression on the narrator. Swann's way epitomizes sexuality and the Guermantes way the aristocracy, two interests he will waste time pursuing in the zigzag path to fulfillment as an artist.

For a moment we return to the adult narrator, in bed, lost in his memories. Then day comes, and with it false impressions disappear. But then, quite suddenly, we are told, in the third person, by an unexpectedly omniscient narrator, of the love affair Swann had with Odette de Crécy before he married her. How the narrator knows so much about every detail of their romance is not explained—possibly he learned all this information from the Baron de Charlus, who was erroneously supposed by the good people of Combray to be Mme Swann's lover, but who actually acted as Swann's watchdog, to keep her lovers away.

Part 2: "Un Amour de Swann" ("Swann in Love")

We have already noticed that the narrator had some personal reasons for having a very awkward approach to love and sex (which in French are traditionally designated by one word, *l'amour*). But the chief point of the "Un Amour de Swann" is that *l'amour* is inseparable from suffering, not just for the narrator, but for everyone. People do not necessarily suffer in marriage, because by then lovers have usually become "just friends," but so long as they are in love they suffer and are jealous. And whoever is the one most in love is at the mercy of the other.

I have heard Proust's view of love described as typically homosexual. Certainly, Thomas Mann, who was also homosexual, endorsed a similar view in "Tonio Kröger"—"Wer am meisten liebt, der ist der Unterlegene und muss leiden" (The one who is most in love is at the other's mercy and must suffer).[8] But for a different reaction we may turn to E. M. Foster, another homosexual, who, while admiring Proust in many ways, strongly disapproved of Proust's pessimistic view of love.[9] My own inclination is to suppose that certain people do experience the emotion of love in terms of suffering and jealousy, but this reaction to love may not have anything to do with their sexual preferences.

Proust may have been wrong to suppose that everyone goes through these negative experiences, but he had quite a store of French literature to back him up. The French have exposed themselves sufficiently to l'amour to be fully aware of its disadvantages. I cannot point to any hero or heroine in Racine's works who is made happy by love, even when it is returned. It is not coincidental that Proust greatly admired Racine (how could he not?). To select a few other French authors whom Proust admired, Choderlos de Laclos, in Les Liaisons dangereuses (Dangerous Affairs), indicates that l'amour leads to disaster, and Flaubert, in Madame Bovary, does the same thing, while Balzac is certainly not celebrated for the happy endings of the love affairs in his novels.

Be this as it may, Swann has a number of happy sensual adventures with women, all of whom provide him with frivolous pleasures, before he experiences the great love of his life for Odette de Crécy, whom he does not initially even consider attractive and yet who makes him suffer abominably. Because of his obsession with her, he is incapable of treating her lightly, as he had treated other women. Proust here sets down his axiom that love, an obsession in the mind, is not based on desire in the body, although the mental obsession often creates the physical desire. This axiom will hold true throughout this great novel, of which "Un Amour de Swann" is generally considered to be a microcosm.

Certain themes are taken up again and amplified, as is the case throughout A la recherche du temps perdu. The themes of the bizarre and the beautiful recur, in the forms of special satire (much more biting than in "Combray"), very cruel humor at the expense of Swann's increasing anguish, and the power of painting and music to charm or to console. But the dominant tone is one of satire. "Un Amour de Swann" begins with a description of the grotesque Verdurin circle, into which Odette brings Swann, who is welcome in far more elevated social circles but who neglects these other circles now for this adventure.

The Verdurins are not accepted either in bourgeois or in aristocratic society, even though they are extremely rich, because they are considered to be artistic bohemians. Their vanity is deeply wounded by this rejection, so they find consolation in claiming that they and their regular guests are superior to the members of any other social group and that it is the people who despise them who are really inferior. Mingled with this theme of wounded vanity is the theme of the conformity required within any social group, a conformity enforced by exclusion from the group for anyone who fails to conform. No one will dispute Proust's observations on the absurdities to which obligatory conformity and wounded vanity give rise, although the modern reader may not fully appreciate the extent to which Swann is demeaning himself by consorting with the Verdurins. However, Swann himself, who treats society merely as a help for his amours, is not particularly conscious of his derogation—at least not to begin with.

The Verdurins supposedly live for art and entertainment. They have a pianist on hand to play their favorite pieces and a painter, M. Biche, also forms part of their company. The painter is a member of the avant-garde, but for the moment we have no idea that he is capable of anything except buffoonery. He will eventually turn out to be one of Proust's *personnages préparés*, that is, people who are eventually revealed to be quite different from what Proust initially leads us to suppose, since he is eventually revealed to be the great artist Elstir. So, even though the Verdurin circle is grotesque, at the same time, it really does have its merits. Proust is far from painting here or elsewhere in black and white. His most appalling characters turn out to have redeeming features, just as his most admirable characters have their blemishes. Professor Brichot, whom Swann despises for his heavyhanded jokes, is erudite and intelligent. Dr. Cottard, another member of the Verdurin circle, who constantly makes absurd puns, will later be revealed as an expert diagnostician. Proust plays a kind of educational game with us designed to make us more hesitant in making value judgments. But he does not excuse the Verdurin's cruelty toward their habitual victim, Saniette.

On the occasion of Swann's first visit to the Verdurins, the pianist plays a sonata that Swann has heard before and that had moved him very deeply, but that he had been unable to identify. It was written by Vinteuil, the obscure music teacher of Combray. But it does not occur to

Swann that this Vinteuil is the same Vinteuil he knows. Here we have another *personnage préparé*, for Vinteuil, who was chiefly associated in "Combray" with his daughter's scandalous love affair, will turn out to be one of the great artists who guide the narrator along the way to creativity and enlightenment.

Vinteuil's sonata very nearly has the same effect on Swann, because he had fallen in love on first hearing with a certain *petite phrase* (little phrase)[10] in the sonata, and it had renewed in his soul, for a while, the artistic sensitivity that had marked his youth but that he had stifled in society. However, Odette, who at that moment is far more interested in Swann than he is in her, takes over the *petite phrase* as the theme song of their relationship, and Swann allows her to do so. Swann begins to fall in love with Odette, just a little, because he transfers his love for the *petite phrase* to her. Here Proust introduces the theme of the betrayal of spiritual values for material ones—a theme that brings Proust very close to the aestheticism of the late nineteenth century.

Proust takes this indication of the superiority of art to life even further when he shows us that Swann, who is a great art connoisseur, begins to see in Odette a likeness to a Botticelli painting and becomes steadily more enamoured as he gazes on a reproduction of this painting. A deep irony is involved, going beyond the profanation of art, because Swann actually uses these adventitious aids quite deliberately in order to fall deeper in love, when, if he knew the misery that awaits him, he would go to great lengths to avoid it. Our blindness to the consequences of our acts is another of Proust's themes. Typically for a Proustian lover, Swann also torments Odette so that she will reveal how much she loves him. For the moment, he is in control. But he will shortly fall much more deeply in love with her than she is with him, and from that moment he will be at her mercy and must suffer the consequences of his servitude. His descent begins one night when Swann arrives at the home of the Verdurins after Odette has left. The sudden rush of anxiety he feels makes him desperate to find her, just as the narrator's desperate longing for his mother's kiss triggered off a state of violent anxiety. When he does eventually run into her, as he searches the streets of Paris, he is entangled in a net of his own making, and that night they make love for the first time. Or rather they "make cattleya," because of the bunch of cattleyas Odette wears in her bosom.

Proust now piles up one satirical detail after another to show that Odette is vulgar, ignorant, and stupid, in order to underline the fact that she is totally unworthy of Swann and that his love for her has no more connection with any basis in reality than any love has. Swann loses touch with reality even further by praising the Verdurins to the skies, simply because, by joining their circle, he can always be sure of meeting Odette. He is in the grip of illusions and lies, as Proust tells us. We all delude ourselves, according to Proust, until we see the light, and many never do see it. Meanwhile Proust has many a hearty laugh, sometimes mingled with tears, at humanity's conceit—since our lies are mainly intended to support the good opinion we have of ourselves—and our folly—for the lies by which we delude ourselves are clearly visible to those who do not share our self-interest. In this respect Proust is very like the seventeenth-century French *moralistes.*

Swann does not realize that he offends the Verdurins' vanity by refusing to accept all their own lies and delusions. A certain Comte de Forcheville does better, and ends up supplanting him. The count also becomes Swann's rival for Odette. But, for the moment, the increasingly besotted Swann can only think of lavishing large sums of money on Odette, without realizing that he is keeping her. However, he does begin to suspect that her motives for remaining his mistress are not altogether disinterested, and it is then that his jealousy begins. There is one absurd scene in which he goes to Odette's house late at night, knocks at some shutters behind which he sees light, and then discovers that he has disturbed her neighbors. There is another in which Swann, having been given a letter by Odette to mail to Forcheville, reads as much of it as he can through the envelope. His jealous suspicions have reduced him to the role of a private detective.

On top of this, the Verdurins exclude him from their circle, in which Forcheville can now meet Odette freely. From then on, Swann lives in almost uninterrupted torment, as he sees Odette less and less and worries more and more about what she is doing behind his back. He is constantly in that state of anxiety that first served to crystallize his love. The more in love he is, the less Odette cares for him, and so on, in an endless chain. He experiences just one moment of relief, when he and Forcheville visit Odette together and Odette treats Swann affectionately in front of Forcheville. But his misery begins again shortly after. He is terrified of displeasing her, and the very fact that he is in love and she is not in love is enough to displease her, so that she is positively annoyed when he comes near her, even though she continues to accept his money. She even has the audacity to ask him to help her rent one of King Ludwig of Bavaria's castles so that she can invite the Verdurins and their circle to attend the Bayreuth Festival with her, while making it clear that he must stay away.

He tries separation a number of times, but cannot carry through. He is the puppet of his love. Proust compares his love to an addiction or a serious illness. But Proust has the idealism to point out the one advantage Swann gains through his suffering: it has completely detached Swann from the superficial, frivolous life he used to lead and has made him open once more to art. Art, wrongly understood, had led Swann into love; love had led to suffering; and suffering now leads Swann back to art. Art, with its integrity and its noble detachment, is for Proust the beginning and the end: all our other preoccupations are mere substitutes. Only a very few human beings, such as the narrator's mother and grandmother, are actually worthy of love. All the others are only good insofar as they ennoble us through the pain they inflict or divert us by their ridiculous behavior. Proust is profoundly disenchanted, but great art is proof against every disenchantment.

Odette tells Swann the most outrageous lies. For example, when the narrator's Uncle Adolphe tries to persuade her to see Swann more often, she accuses him to Swann of attempted rape, and for once Swann believes her. But it is not long before Swann is once more deeply engaged in the difficult and exhausting business of trying to find out what she is concealing from him. The narrator will later go through the same process with his girlfriend, Albertine. Proust's heroes spend much more time and energy in trying to know their lady loves intellectually than carnally. It is at this moment that Swann calls upon his friend, M. de Charlus, to watch over Odette. M. de Charlus, who will take on enormous importance in the novel as it proceeds, is homosexual, even though Proust does not choose to be explicit about this just yet. So he is a safe companion for Odette, and can relieve Swann of the need to imagine what she is doing, which is such a strain that it makes him long for death. He can only endure his misery by deliberately forgetting that there was a time when Odette was in love with him. But there comes a time when he is forced to remember.

He goes one evening to a musical entertainment given by the Marquise de Saint-Euverte. He is so detached by his suffering from the ordinary, frivolous, social preoccupations that his aesthetic perceptions are greatly heightened and he sees the Marquise's domestics in terms of one great painting after another. He had always had a tendency to identify people with paintings, but only in a superficial way. Now he actually has the vision of an artist, and continues to have it while he moves among the other male guests, who seem much uglier to him than the servants, but equally remarkable. He is seeing creatively for the first time in years. So the suffering induced by love is good for something.

For the first time in *A la recherche du temps perdu* we enter the world of the aristocracy, that world from which the Verdurins so much resent being excluded. Now we find that, apart from the fact that there are certain aristocrats, such as Mme des Laumes (who is to become the Duchesse de Guermantes), whom no one would dream of excluding, the reciprocal game of exclusion, designed to heighten the self-importance of the excluder, goes on here too. And the aristocrats are, in their own way, just as absurd as the Verdurins and their circle. For instance, Mme des Laumes imitates Mme de Cambremer senior by beating time to the music, but in order to assert her independence, does so out of time. She makes a scatological joke at the expense of the Cambremers (presumably in order to compensate for having followed the example of an inferior), which is more original than any Dr. Cottard would have made, but just as stupid and vulgar. And she sneers at the Jénas because they are recent nobles. But Swann does not notice her flaws because he is a member of her group and because within this group Mme des Laumes is renowned for her wit. However, he does feel that he is surrounded by stupid and ridiculous people, and he would have left before the end if he could have done so politely.

As it happens, the last piece of music on the programme is the Vinteuil sonata, although Swann did not know this beforehand. In fact he does not even recognize it until the *petite phrase* makes its appearance, because the *petite phrase* had become the only part of the sonata that he knew. It fulfills the requirements of an involuntary memory although it is neither gustatory, olfactory, nor tactile, because it has strong emotional associations, and because, since Odette is no longer interested in catering to him, he has not heard it for some time. It immediately brings back memories of the happy days when Odette was in love with him. This does not bring him happiness, at first, but only acute pain. But then he begins to listen to the *petite phrase* itself, and he falls in love with it once more. It has a lesson to teach him of smiling resignation, and he accepts it. It seems like a divinity whose call makes even death less bitter. Proust describes the wonder of the Vinteuil sonata at length, placing it in a supernatural realm. Vinteuil is revealed as a genius of the first rank, and Swann is at this moment at the peak of his existence.

However, his love does not disappear; he simply loses hope, a change revealed in his dreams. He sees himself as someone else, whom he tries to counsel and comfort. But this does not prevent him from being jealous. When he gets an anonymous letter saying that Odette is not only promiscuous but has also had many lesbian love affairs and frequents brothels, he starts to question her. At first he totally disbelieves the last two allegations, but then he is horrified to discover that all the accusations are true. This scene, in which a lover jealously questions a beloved of whose sexual orientation he disapproves, is typically Proustian. The narrator will go even further with Albertine, in *La Prisonnière* and *La Fugitive,* but Albertine, who is far more sensitive than Odette, will admit far less than Odette, who is simply irritated by Swann's attitude. Swann is the one who suffers, not Odette, for he discovers that she was behaving in this way even during what he had believed to be the happy days of their love.

He starts going to brothels to see if anyone there knows Odette, but he is saved from this vain pursuit when the Verdurins suddenly buy a yacht and take their entire circle with them on a long cruise. Some of the travelers come back before the others, and Swann runs into one of them, Mme Cottard, on a bus. Mme Cottard tells him how Odette has been praising him throughout the cruise. Hearing this, his jealousy, his anxiety, and his love all disappear together. Since Proustian emotion is cyclical, these emotions reappear in a dream, from which Swann awakes to hurry off to an assignation with Mme de Cambremer, Jr., marveling as he goes at the absurdity of having suffered so much for a woman who was not his type. As a view of the nobility and permanence of love, this could hardly be more cynical. Swann will, in fact, marry Odette, but only for the sake of their daughter, of whom we shall shortly hear more. But Proust does not tell us exactly when and how this marriage takes place. We only know that Gilberte and the narrator are approximately the same age.

Part 3: "Noms de Pays: Le Nom" ("Place Names: The Name")

Quite suddenly, with the disregard for conventional transition that characterizes *Du côté de chez Swann*, we are back in the bedroom where the narrator spent his sleepless nights remembering other bedrooms in which he slept or did not sleep. Now he remembers the one he inhabited in the Grand Hôtel de la Plage at Balbec. But he does not dwell on it. Instead he returns to his boyhood, in Paris this time, and his dreams of

Balbec. His imagination has been inflamed by the highly poetic descriptions of Legrandin, which were calculated to make this literary lad think of Balbec as a place that was both literary and yet real at the same time. And Swann had reinforced this preoccupation by saying that the church of Balbec was gothic and Persian at the same time. In other words, the narrator is in love—with a place that is as strongly individualized as a person and just as distorted by romantic dreams.

At the same time, with an inconstancy that causes no trouble in dreams, he is also in love with Florence, Parma, and Venice, because he is intended to visit northern Italy at Easter. Because of Italian paintings and because of Ruskin's writings, these cities are pictures themselves, and all in color. After that thought he switches to thoughts of Brittany and Normandy and runs through a whole litany of names that he takes as phonetic representations of the towns themselves. Then he goes back in thought to Venice and Florence again. In other words, he is attempting to arrive at reality by the use of his active imagination, as he will do for the rest of his life whenever his emotions are involved, instead of by testing reality directly. He has got worse since the early days in Combray. He still has the old problem of not being able to make contact, but now it is even worse. This problem will plague him all his life, cause him endless torment and disappointment, and eventually force him to enter a sanatorium. But for the moment it simply gives him a fever that prevents him from going anywhere except to the Champs-Elysées with Françoise, whom the family has inherited from Aunt Léonie. As in the *drame du coucher*, Proust is somewhere between laughter and tears as he tells us on what bubbles the narrator's joys are based and how soon they burst.

However, in the Champs-Elysées, where he is taken to play with the other children—they appear to be quite big children by this time, probably about age 12 or 13—he encounters Gilberte Swann for the second time and becomes her favorite playmate. He falls desperately in love with her and treasures her tokens of affection: an agate marble and a brochure on Racine by Bergotte. He also seizes every opportunity to talk about the Swanns and their house, because in his thoughts they have become supernatural beings who inhabit a magical residence. Unfortunately, the real Gilberte is disappointing compared to the Gilberte he conjures up in his imagination, and she does not prefer his company to everyone else. This absurd and heartrending adventure will continue throughout the first half of the subsequent part of the narrative, *A l'ombre des jeunes filles en fleurs*. But before we enter the enchanted garden of the *jeunes filles en fleurs*, Proust concludes *Du côté de chez Swann* with a walk in the Bois de Boulogne, which is the enchanted garden of women. Preeminent among these women is Mme Swann, a vision of high fashion, reclining in her carriage and replying to the greetings of her lovers, past and present. But this concluding section, which contrasts the all-too attainable mother with the unattainable daughter, switches suddenly to a much later time when the narrator haunts the Bois de Boulogne in search of the past and finds only shadows of what had been.

Chapter Three
A l'ombre des jeunes filles en fleurs (*Within a Budding Grove*)

Part 1 "Autour de Mme Swann"
("Madame Swann at Home")

With his characteristic mixture of laughter and tears, Proust takes us from the melancholy that reigned at the end of *Du côté de chez Swann* to a scene of comedy, with the dinner invitation that the narrator's parents extend to the Marquis de Norpois, a diplomat who speaks entirely in old-fashioned political clichés. Proust was fascinated by the comic effects to be found in idiosyncratic ways of speaking. Elsewhere, Legrandin arouses the family's mirth by using elevated poetical language to conceal his real interests and Bloch consistently uses a jargon of his own invention to increase—so he hopes—his prestige.

But before Monsieur de Norpois arrives, we learn, to our astonishment, that the narrator's parents would not dream of inviting Swann to be a fellow guest, because of his vulgar habit of boasting about his social connections. However, they are seriously thinking of inviting Dr. Cottard, because he is an eminent scientist. Seeing Swann and Cottard through the parents' eyes both reveals these two characters from a new perspective and brings us up short with the realization of the changes that time can work—for time is the fourth dimension of Proust's great novel as of the church of Combray.

However, Monsieur de Norpois, not content with being a close colleague of the narrator's father, had taken it on himself to intervene in the narrator's life by saying that he should be allowed to see the great actress, Berma, whom the boy had previously been prevented from seeing because such excitement would have been too much for his nervous system. The narrator has already been exposed to Berma in two acts of *Phèdre* by the time the Marquis arrives for dinner. Unfortunately, he is unable to say that he enjoyed the performance.

His imagination, which throughout the book plays the role of a wicked fairy, cursing him with the inability to enjoy anything that does not happen just as he had imagined it beforehand, causes him to be disappointed by Berma's simple, natural acting style, for he had anticipated a highly refined style. He had expected to see an actress and he had seen Phèdre in person. However, he cannot explain the nature of his disappointment to his irritated father or to Monsieur de Norpois because he does not understand it himself. In all humility, he seeks correction, but Monsieur de Norpois does not give him much to go on.

In fact, Monsieur de Norpois's total incompetence as a literary critic is revealed by the absurdity of his advice to the narrator to model himself on a young man who has proved his talent by writing a study on the sense of the infinite on the west bank of Lake Victoria and another on the use of the repeating rifle in the Bulgarian army. Monsieur de Norpois even encourages the narrator to seek this author's advice. But when the narrator shows him a piece of his own writing—probably the one about the steeples of Martinville—Monsieur de Norpois refrains from praising it. It might possibly have been more to the point to ask the opinion of Françoise, who has a true appreciation of genius because as a cook she is a genius herself.

After a disquisition on Swann's marriage to Odette and on the pride and joy Swann feels if anyone respectable is willing to visit her—a disquisition that comes partly from Monsieur de Norpois and partly from one of the narrator's older voices, as the critic Marcel Muller might say[1]—Monsieur de Norpois mentions that he had met Bergotte at the Swanns'. Monsieur de Norpois condemns Bergotte and at the same time condemns the piece of writing that the narrator had shown him and which was obviously inspired by Bergotte. Bergotte disgusts Monsieur de Norpois because of the depravity of his private life, which contradicts the moralizing tone of his books, and his lack of social usefulness.

At this point, it is worth mentioning that Proust himself firmly stated that there is no necessary connection between a great author's private life and his work.[2] We will hear more about this idea in the second part of *A l'ombre des jeunes filles en fleurs*, but it will suffice for the moment to say that the contrast between how Charles Dickens lived with his own family and the way he wrote about family life, for example, or the contrast between Thomas Hardy's cruelty toward the women he knew and the sensitivity with which he wrote about fictional women, seems to prove the truth of Proust's assertion. It is taking altogether too narrow a view of the matter to suppose that Proust made this distinction simply and solely to keep people from discussing his homosexuality.

The narrator turns the conversation onto Mme Swann and Gilberte and makes such a passionate declaration of the gratitude he would feel if Monsieur de Norpois would put him in touch with Mme Swann that the old diplomat makes up his mind to do nothing of the sort. This is a typical example of the way in which the narrator puts obstacles in his own path by letting himself get carried away by his emotions. His tendency to emotional extremes is another wicked fairy in league with his imagination. However much they may help him in his solitary joys, they are a hindrance to him in any kind of material success. Eventually, Dr. Cottard, who will be called in to cure the narrator's asthmatic attacks, will put the narrator in touch with Mme Swann—not because he intends to do the narrator a favor, but because he thinks that this action will prove useful to himself.

In the meantime, the narrator writes to Gilberte to say that their friendship should get off to a new start with the New Year, and begins to meet her once more at the Champs-Elysées. But now she tells him that her parents are not particularly keen on him. Then, quite suddenly, the narrator is distracted from Gilberte by a moment of true happiness quite different from the emotional fever into which he is plunged by her presence. How does this come about? He walks into a public lavatory and is delighted by the damp, musty smell. Proust does not comment on this occurrence immediately, but it becomes clear to the reader that the narrator is undergoing an involuntary memory, one connected with his uncle Adolphe's room at Combray. Just for a moment fate gives him a little nudge, pointing him in his true direction, but only for a moment. He reverts to Gilberte, and even to a form of sexual contact with her leading to orgasm as they wrestle for possession of his New Year's letter.

But then he falls ill and is not able to visit the Champs-Elysées for a while. Gilberte writes to him, just as he had wished, to invite him to her house. The narrator deduces from this event that sometimes one's wishes are gratified in the most surprising way, just when one had got used to seeing them denied. The cosmic kaleidoscope gives a turn, far beyond one's anticipation, and what was impossible becomes real. I think Proust means to suggest that everything that happens is a question of cause and effect, but that we are surprised by the effects because we do not know all the causes. One cause that will find its effect much later in the novel is that Gilberte has such an affected and elaborate signature that her name can be read as Albertine, the name of the narrator's later love. But for the moment, since neither the narrator nor the reader has the gift of prophecy, Gilberte's elaborate signature means nothing. It seems to be just one more of the many apparently insignificant details that the narrator mentions in passing; only in retrospect do we discover that these details are part of a carefully planned structure.

When the narrator goes to visit Gilberte he is in a state of rapture that puts him beside himself. Everything seems magical to him. He drinks quantities of tea, forgetting that it makes him ill, and he is so over-whelmed by Swann's kindness that he cannot understand a word he says. But he is capable of taking in the names of Mme Swann's visitors, such as Mme Bontemps, the aunt of Albertine, in a critical spirit reinforced by his mother's sarcasms on the subject of their low social level.

Swann, no longer in love with Odette but simply fond of her, is happy about anything that will make his wife happy. Moreover, people's social standing, Proust goes on to point out, is no more stable than anything else in this world of constant change. The society of Mme Bontemps is the best Swann can hope for his wife at this particular moment, although a few of his aristocratic friends—chiefly men—still visit him. He can introduce her to the Prince d'Agrigente but not to the Duchesse de Guermantes, which is something he longs to do. And he and Mme Swann are at pains to please the narrator, in whom they possibly see, although Proust does not say so, a suitable future husband for Gilberte.

Mme Swann entertains the narrator by playing the part of the Vinteuil sonata that contains the little phrase. This phrase no longer has the power to touch Swann to the heart with memories of his lost love; now it simply makes him remember the Verdurins. The mediocre happiness for which he has settled has destroyed all memory of the suffering that at one time raised him to a higher aesthetic plane. But what is the end of a true appreciation of Vinteuil's music for Swann is the beginning for the narrator, even if it is only the beginning.

The Swanns also take the narrator out for walks with them. On one of these walks they meet the Princesse Mathilde, the niece of Napoleon, who chats about the celebrities she has known. The boy who had dreamed hopelessly of meeting the Duchesse de Guermantes now finds himself quite casually in contact with a great lady whom he had not even thought of meeting. Because he had not imagined such a meeting, he does not seem to react with any particular emotion even to Mme Swann's suggestion that it would be possible for him to pay the Princesse a visit. With the Princesse Mathilde, he had entered by the gate of horn, the gate through which true dreams come in the *Odyssey* and the *Aeneid*, not the gate of ivory through which deluding dreams come.

But while Gilberte's parents do not lose an opportunity to be agreeable to the narrator, Gilberte herself, whose kindness and considerateness have been praised by her parents, suddenly shows a completely different side to her nature. She had told the narrator that she would stay with her father on the anniversary of his father's death, but when the day actually comes she insists on going to a concert, and gets really angry with the narrator when he tries to make her stay home. For the moment this inconsistency seems inexplicable, but later the narrator will explain to us that Gilberte, being a mixture of her father and her mother, will behave and talk sometimes like one and sometimes like the other, leaving the narrator wondering if she is one person or twins. These contradictions in people's characters are an endless source of fascination for the narrator, and he will give us many other examples. For instance, the fact that Françoise can be both cruel and kind was already indicated in "Combray." And the same thing will prove true of Bergotte, whom the narrator meets at a luncheon party given by Mme Swann.

As a boy in Combray the narrator had dreamed that he would get to know Gilberte, and that she would introduce him to her friend Bergotte. This dream is actually realized now, at the moment when he least expects it, although it is Odette, not Gilberte, who effects the introduction. Proust is considered by many of his readers to be a pessimistic writer because he is so convinced that love can only lead to suffering. But in a sense he is a very optimistic writer: how else can we explain why so many of the narrator's dreams come true? It happens quite frequently, of course, that he is completely taken aback by the way in which his dreams come true. In a Tarot reading, getting the wish card does not always mean that the wish that is to be fulfilled will make one as happy as one expects. Thus the narrator gets a very real shock when he is introduced to Bergotte and discovers that the famous writer is not the gentle, white-haired, old singer of his dreams, but a short, vulgar-looking young man with a black goatee and a red nose in the shape of a snailshell.

The narrator does not seem particularly concerned by what Monsieur de Norpois had said about Bergotte's immorality. Whether he disbelieved it or considered it irrelevant, Proust does not tell us. But the conversation, as well as the appearance, of Bergotte does strike him as disconcerting because he cannot at first seek the connection between the man and his books. One of the narrator's older voices takes over and explains to the reader, at some length, what the connection is, and also makes it clear how conversation differs from written style. For one thing, Bergotte is charmed by certain words, such as "visage," which he pronounces in a very exaggerated manner but which he knows how to

situate in his text in a way that will give the word its true value. For
another, he is very fond of images, and uses so many of them in
conversation, while pronouncing them all on the same note, that his
spoken manner seems emphatic, pretentious, and monotonous all at
once. He is incapable of talking otherwise and would address a judge, if
he were taken to court, in the same way.

Certain elements of his spoken manner he owes partly to a friend of his
and partly to his brothers and sisters. But those who would be liable to
despise the vulgarity of Bergotte's family would be like the owners of
Rolls Royces who might sneer at Bergotte's modest vehicle without
realizing that it is an airplane that can soar far above them. Vulgar he
certainly is, because he makes unpleasant remarks about the Swanns, who
are old friends of his, the minute he leaves their house. And he can treat
people extremely badly, just as he can be surprisingly generous and kind.
But what seems to make the greatest impression on the narrator is what
Bergotte says about Berma in *Phèdre*. He disagrees with the narrator, and
yet accepts the latter's point of view in a way Monsieur de Norpois had
shown himself incapable of doing.

This, in itself, would do nothing to reverse the bad opinion that the
narrator's parents, relying on Monsieur de Norpois, have formed of
Bergotte, but they suddenly begin to approve of him when they learn
that he thinks their son is intelligent. The narrator himself is surprised
when Bergotte tells him that his chief joys must be those of the mind,
since he is aware that his greatest recent joy had come from experiencing
the smell of a public washroom. As if to prove the truth of the narrator's
lack of intellectual interests, the narrator's next move will be to accompany Bloch to a brothel, at which he meets a Jewish prostitute named
Rachel who will figure largely in the narrative much further on.

But, with his usual tendency to engage in self-defeating gambits,
he seems to have done nothing in the brothel except talk and make the
madam a present of some of his Aunt Léonie's furniture. Feeling that he
has desecrated his aunt's memory by this action, he does not go back to
the brothel. But he sells more of his aunt's furniture, as well as her
silverware, in order to send flowers to Mme Swann, not realizing how
valuable the silverware would be to him later on or how uninteresting
Mme Swann would seem by then. In connection with his enthusiasm for
Gilberte and her parents, he pronounces one of the axioms that become
more frequent in his work as it progresses: "Ce n'est jamais qu'à cause
d'un état d'esprit qui n'est pas destiné à durer qu'on prend des résolutions
définitives" (It is always because of a state of mind that is not destined to

last that one makes permanent resolutions).[3] The follies of the callow younger narrator supply the wisdom of the older one.

Another of his follies, at this particular moment, is to suppose that he can become a great writer not by shutting himself up alone to write but by dining with Mme Swann in the company of Bergotte. But his chief folly is to suppose that the pressure the Swanns put on Gilberte to devote herself to the narrator will guarantee her interest in him, when in fact the reverse is the case. Gilberte comes to feel more and more resentment at the way this difficult admirer is being forced on her, a resentment that she finally directs at the narrator himself. Seeing this, the narrator, unable to bear his disappointment, devotes all his willpower to separating himself from Gilberte, much as Swann, with far less success, had attempted to separate himself from Odette.

But the narrator, becoming more manipulative as he grows older, does not have the intention of destroying his own love, although that is the ultimate unforeseen result, so much as that of renewing Gilberte's love for him by showing that he can do without her. Consequently, he continues to visit Mme Swann, at hours when he knows Gilberte will be out. A long description of Mme Swann and her salon follows, interspersed with accounts of the narrator's struggle not to yield to the impulses of his love. But what puts the finishing touch to his despair is the sight of Gilberte and a young man walking down the Champs-Elysées, just when he thought his maneuver had succeeded. "The young man" will turn out to be the lesbian actress Léa in men's clothing. But not in the Flammarion edition. Even Gilberte has to be suspected of lesbianism at some point. However, the narrator becomes more and more interested in Mme Swann, her flowers and her dresses, and, like *Du côté de chez Swann*, this part ends with an evocation of Mme Swann in the Bois de Boulogne.

Part 2 "Noms de pays: le pays" ("Place Names: the Place")

Here begins the most fateful and at the same time the most beautiful and the most joyous of the episodes in the narrator's life, if we except his childhood in Combray. The narrator, who by now has almost completely succeeded in becoming indifferent to Gilberte, not to mention her parents, sets off on a visit to Balbec, a seaside resort in Normandy on which he has lavished as many dreams as on Gilberte and Bergotte. The apparently random encounters he will make in Balbec will shape the rest of his life. Proust's notion of casuality will once more be at work, with the random scattering of causes producing certain definite, determined effects on the narrator.

He and his grandmother take the train together, but part company during their journey so that he can see the church of Balbec, which he has longed to see ever since he had heard it described as almost Persian by Swann. His mother sees them off, making the narrator so unhappy over their separation that he becomes slightly drunk in order to deal with his emotions. His grandmother gives him Mme de Sévigné to read, and he is struck by what he calls her Dostoyevsky side—that is, the way she describes things in terms of her immediate impressions, without any logical explanation. Later in his journey he admires the sunrise and a good-looking young country girl who brings café au lait to the train. He seems to be completely reconciled to the journey. But his view of the church of Balbec, which, contrary to his dreams, is situated at some distance from the sea, disappoints him by its materiality. It is not a fairy-tale church but a real one, and that diminishes it in his eyes. His disappointment is, of course, the work of the wicked fairy Imagination.

Having rejoined his grandmother, he arrives at the Grand Hotel of Balbec, where the narrator finds himself intimidated and alarmed to a comic degree by everyone and everything around him, including his room. But his grandmother, knowing and loving him as she does, comes to his rescue. The narrator, deeply touched by her immense love for him, a love he seeks to duplicate outside his family circle but never finds, is so moved by the way she comes into his room to reassure him that he clings to her and hangs on her cheek like a child at the breast. Hers is the next room, and she tells him to knock three times on the partition wall if he needs anything. His happiness when she responds to his knock destroys his anxiety, and next morning he is able to rejoice at the sight of the sea, of which literature has fortunately not given him a false impression. In fact, the sight of the sun on the sea gives him a better understanding of "Chant d'automne" by Baudelaire.

The narrator's ready interest in those around him makes him take notice of the other guests in the Grand Hotel, particularly when they gather in the dining room. One little group of Norman notables attracts his attention from the start. Uncertain that people will recognize their importance, they cast disparaging glances at most of the other guests and make even more disparaging comments, particularly the women in the party. They are provincial examples of the tendency that Proust sees everywhere in society to push other people down in order to increase one's own stature. Those who are willing to treat all comers as their equals do exist, but they are rare. And this little group of notables will form a kind of comic, backbiting chorus to the comings and goings at the Grand Hotel.

Unfamiliar with the world of the highest aristocracy, they lump together in their disdain the "king" and "queen" of a Pacific isle, a rich young man who is addicted to gambling, and an aristocratic old lady who has brought her entourage with her to the hotel and who knows that it would be useless to try to make her fellow guests understand the position she occupies in Paris. Guests accepted and admired by the Norman notables include M. de Stermaria, who is full of family pride, and his daughter, and M. de Cambremer, who is Legrandin's brother-in-law. Also staying at the Grand Hotel are a little group of friends who spend all their time playing cards, ignoring everyone and everything else.

Outside, the poor people of Balbec gaze in at this "aquarium," into which they may break some day and eat the "fish"—a revolutionary speculation that comes as a surprise from an author who is generally supposed to be a snob. Certainly, the narrator himself is far from despising those around him and would like to get to know them. He takes a particular fancy, in his flighty way, to Mlle de Stermaria, just as he had fancied the girl who brought coffee to the train. All he lacks to be a Casanova is physical endurance, but most of his fancies are fleeting and come to nothing, or else turn into neurotic emotional obsessions. In a similar way, all he needs to be a true democrat is to get rid of his anxious concern with other people's opinions—a concern unknown to his grandmother.

The aristocratic old lady turns out to be the Marquise de Villeparisis, an old schoolfriend of the narrator's grandmother. The narrator would like to be introduced to her, so as to make an impression on Mlle de Stermaria, but in fact the two old ladies prefer to leave each other alone until contact becomes unavoidable. Eventually they do renew their friendship, but this event has not the slightest effect on the narrator's other social connections—at any rate, none until Mme de Villeparisis introduces him to two members of her family, the Marquis Robert de Saint-Loup and the Baron de Charlus. But this will happen much later, and will have no effect on the other guests in the Grand Hotel, any more than will her introduction of the narrator and his grandmother to the Princesse de Luxembourg. In any case, the little chorus of notables thinks the Princesse de Luxembourg is a courtesan, which definitely lowers the

Marquise de Villeparisis in their opinion. For Proust there is not one
Capital-S Society, but a series of little societies, all very pleased with
themselves and ignorant of each other, insofar as they are not actively
jealous of each other.

However, Mme de Villeparisis turns out to have an unexpected fund of
information concerning the narrator's father, who does not belong in any
way to the Marquise's world but who is traveling in Spain with Monsieur
de Norpois, her longtime lover. Naturally, she does not give this
explanation.

In spite of the narrator's love of the sea, on which he gazes eagerly from
his bedroom window, a local doctor decides that it is bad for the narrator
to spend all his time on the beach. The Marquise de Villeparisis offers to
take the narrator and his grandmother for drives in the surrounding
countryside. He eagerly takes in the beauty offered to him on these
drives, but feels distinctly skeptical when Mme de Villeparisis proceeds
to denigrate the authors Chateaubriand, Balzac, Hugo, Stendhal, Vigny,
and Musset, many of whom she had known personally, because of their
social gaucherie and their personal absurdities. The narrator feels very
strongly that the people who know best how to behave in society lack
genius. She even quotes Sainte-Beuve in support of her opinion that
knowing the man gives a more accurate idea of his work, which, of
course, considering Proust's objections to Sainte-Beuve, indicates con-
clusively that the Marquise's opinion is of no value.

But the narrator's thoughts are not only on literature, for since Bloch
had told him that all women and girls are eager to make love, he covets
every girl he sees passing by, and even goes to some trouble to convince
a girl he finds fishing from a bridge that he is an important person, so
that he can be sure that he has made an impression on her. When he is in
this mood he is totally preoccupied by sensual pleasure. Thus when he
gets a letter from Bergotte, he is disappointed that it has not come from
a dairymaid in whom he is taking an interest.

On one of these drives, however, something far more profound than
sensual attraction or critical intelligence speaks to him. As they go down
toward Hudimesnil, he sees three trees that give him the profound sense
of happiness that he has seldom felt since Combray. He is obviously
experiencing a case of involuntary memory. But it remains incomplete,
because he cannot identify its origin or meaning. He is in despair over
this difficulty, even to the extent of feeling like a renegade. His failure is
a betrayal of what is truly essential to him. If only he had been alone, he
believes, he could have grasped what the trees had to tell him and that

insight would have made him truly happy. But the carriage carries him away from happiness, like his life.

For someone who has an ultimate vocation for solitude, the narrator spends a great deal of time in company, and in particular in the company of people who do not and cannot satisfy him. This is a tragicomic error that he will not overcome until he is nearly too old to do anything about it. What complicates the narrator's dilemma is that he can only utilize the past, for the present is something too fleeting for him to grasp. The wish for total possession bedevils him and he can only possess in totality something that exists in the past and the present at the same time. He is a container that is only happy when it has something to contain and is contained in its turn in a larger container, as his grandmother's love contains him. There is a connection between this idea of the contained container and the passage in "Combray" on the water jugs dipped into the Vivonne which has aroused much critical interest. Gérard Genette's remarks on this passage, in which he establishes the contiguity of the Proustian metaphor, are particularly striking.[4]

Back at the hotel, the Marquise de Villeparisis showers the grandmother and the narrator with loans of books, gifts of fruit, and anecdotes about life in society. But her attentions do not prevent the narrator from expressing a low opinion of her critical judgment. His grandmother, in contrast, would like to see him adopting the Marquise's attitudes, for the sake of his happiness in life. But fairly soon the conversation turns to the topic of the grandmother's death, for she is bound to die before the narrator, and whether the narrator will be happy without her. Seeing that his grandmother desires his happiness above all else, he seeks to console her.

But this moment of sadness passes, like all other moments, and the narrator is quickly distracted by the sight of the Marquise's nephew, the Marquis Robert de Saint-Loup-en-Bray. He cuts such a dashing, handsome, and elegant figure that the narrator immediately wishes to become his friend and is distressed to hear that he is passionately in love with a wicked woman who, the narrator supposes, will shortly bring him to a bad end. The Marquis de Saint-Loup's preliminary manner toward the narrator is extremely distant, but to the narrator's great surprise the young Marquis actually does want to become his friend. Once more, the narrator's wishes are being granted in the most surprising way. This time his interest in literature and the other arts works in his favor, for Robert de Saint-Loup rates the arts far higher than the prestige of the aristocracy. Saint-Loup turns out to be the most kind and considerate of friends, but with his usual contrariness the narrator decides that he does not enjoy this friendship as much as he thought he would, because he prefers to be alone.

Suddenly, when the narrator is sitting on the beach with Saint-Loup, the ubiquitous Bloch bobs up, like a Hyde to the narrator's Jekyll. Bloch is as remarkable for vulgarity and lack of tact as Saint-Loup is for refinement. And yet the narrator seems equally fond of them both. He seems to value people simply for being very strongly what they are. Thus, he is disappointed that Saint-Loup is not more of an aristocrat and less of an intellectual. But Bloch, not worried in the least by these distinctions, attaches himself to Saint-Loup, apparently solely because of his title, and then insults the narrator by calling him a social climber because he got to know Saint-Loup first. After that, Bloch invites Saint-Loup and the narrator to dinner with his family, in the hope of doing a little social climbing himself. But the two dinner guests have to put off the invitation because Saint-Loup is expecting his uncle Palamède, whom he praises to the skies.

The narrator actually sees this uncle staring at him next day, in front of the casino, in such an odd way that he thinks he must be a crook or a madman. Consequently, he is surprised to meet this "madman" a little later in the company of Mme de Villeparisis and Robert de Saint-Loup and hear him introduced as the Baron de Charlus, a member of the Guermantes family. The narrator is thrilled by this mention of the Guermanteses, since he had daydreamed about the Duchesse de Guermantes back in Combray. At this point, the narrator's denial that he is a social climber seems a little less certain.

Be that as it may, he finds the Baron de Charlus most intriguing, while the Baron seems equally intrigued by him, for reasons that will only become apparent much later. We soon learn that it is the oddity of the Baron's manner and behavior rather than his connection with the Duchesse de Guermantes that really intrigues the narrator. His grandmother, on the other hand, is deeply touched by the sensibility with which the Baron speaks of her favorite author, Mme de Sévigné, as well as of Racine and La Fontaine. And although the narrator is astonished by the Baron's sudden, unexpected changes of attitude, he gathers in the long run that he has made a favorable impression, without understanding how or why. This is the kind of thing that he meant when he spoke of the Dostoyevsky side of Mme de Sévigné, in that she described her impressions without explaining them.

After this, Saint-Loup and the narrator go to dine with Bloch's family, and the narrator takes great pleasure in showing that they are ignorant, pretentious, and vulgar. Proust has an anti-Semitic side, in spite of his love and respect for his Jewish mother, and his anti-Semitism comes out when he writes of Bloch and his relations. But by way of concealing his own anti-Semitism, Proust makes Bloch a Jewish anti-Semite, as well as someone who is so totally impervious to other people's feelings that he insults the Baron de Charlus to Saint-Loup and asks the narrator for the name of Mme Swann, saying in front of everybody that he had made love to her in a train without knowing who she was.

Naturally enough, this dinner party does not bring Bloch and Saint-Loup closer together. The narrator goes on to talk about Saint-Loup's mistress, an aspiring actress who has stimulated Saint-Loup's intellectual ambitions, but has come to dislike him because she thinks he is damaging her career. Poor Saint-Loup suffers from her disdain, in a pattern familiar to us by this time, and spends most of his time sending her telegrams and letters in order to stave off the day when she will finally leave him.

However, uppermost in the narrator's mind a few days after the dinner with Bloch is his grandmother's delight at being photographed by Saint-Loup. Without realizing for a moment that she is ill and wants to have a photograph of herself to leave her grandson as a memorial of her, he is so unpleasant to her about it that her pleasure is quite spoiled. But he is so selfish that he feels ill-treated. He wants to be loved, but he does not know how to love. The narrator is very candid with us about his faults; this is one of the ways in which he makes us feel close to him, for we all have painful memories of this kind.

There is a little space in the text to allow this memory to recede, and then we are presented with a most important event: the narrator's sight of the group of wild young hoydens who are generally known to Proustians as the *petite bande* (the little band). This group of girls comes strolling along the promenade, forcing everyone to get out of their way, and one of them even jumps right over a feeble old gentleman who is sitting by the promenade on a deckchair, while another makes sarcastic remark about him. The narrator, who equates cruelty in a Nietzschean way with energy and health, is fascinated and enchanted, and from that moment on his chief concern is to be accepted into the *petite bande*.

Proust acknowledged to Gide that all his beautiful memories of male partners in his homosexual affairs had been attributed in his novel to young girls.[5] When he shows us a group of girls doing things that only boys might have done at the historical time described, he does stretch our credulity. Albertine, the member of the *petite bande* who will have the most importance for the narrator, is definitely not a *jeune fille* according to the ideas of 1918. Because the *petite bande* as a whole is so outrageous, the narrator thinks that any member of it should be "easy to get," and that is the kind of girl he is looking for.

The narrator, who is no laggard when it comes to things he really wants to do, goes back to the hotel, and starts making inquiries about the Simonet family, since he has overheard a remark that leads him to believe that Simonet is the surname of one of the members of the *petite bande*. He is informed that there is a Simonet family in Balbec. He tries to get Saint-Loup to go looking for the *petite bande*, but fails to enlist his cooperation because Saint-Loup is too preoccupied with his actress. So they go off regularly to have dinner together at Rivebelle. There the narrator gets into such a euphoric state under the influence of alcohol that everything around him seems enchanted, he becomes indifferent to the *petite bande*, and he even loses all concern for his life on the return journey.

On one of these visits to the restaurant in Rivebelle, they make the acquaintance of the famous painter Elstir. They have never heard of him before, but on learning that he is famous they are very eager to meet him. Elstir invites the narrator to visit him in his studio. But soon after, the narrator has fresh hopes of contacting the *petite bande*, and the idea of getting to know Elstir no longer seems so appealing. However, at his grandmother's urging, he does go, but without much enthusiasm. Once he gets inside Elstir's studio, he is thrilled. There are no examples of Elstir's first and second manners, in which he was influenced by mythology (like Gustave Moreau) and by the art of Japan (like several of the impressionists), both of which are well represented in the collection of the Duchesse de Guermantes. The studio is filled with metaphorical seascapes painted at Balbec. Proust was deeply impressed by the power of the metaphor, so he makes his narrator fascinated by the metaphors in these seascapes, particularly one outstanding one, *Le Port de Carquethuit*, which renders the sea in terms of the land and the land in terms of the sea. It is generally accepted that Proust's Elstir is a compendium of Whistler, Turner, and the impressionists in general, and that Proust was envisioning Turner in particular at this point.

As well as being a great artist, Elstir is a well-informed art historian. He explains the beauties of the church of Balbec which had completely escaped the narrator. He even explains what is Persian about it. He is also a psychologist and a philosopher, because he explains to the narrator that someone who is inclined to be dreamy needs to go right through his dreams in order to get to know them.

But then suddenly a member of the *petite bande* passes by the house, and the narrator realizes that this girl is a friend of Elstir's. She is the Mlle Simonet he has been looking for—Albertine Simonet, the Albertine for whom he will have his greatest love. Elstir knows the entire *petite bande*, so the narrator asks him to go out with him for a walk in the hope of meeting them. But before they leave the narrator finds an old picture of Elstir's that the latter hides from his wife; the picture portrays a woman dressed much like a man. The narrator and Elstir go out, and they do meet members of the *petite bande*, but the narrator suddenly gets into a nervous state and remains at a distance while Elstir talks to these girls. He is waiting for Elstir to call to him to join them, but Elstir does not. The narrator thinks that the girls had prevented Elstir from inviting him to join them.

To make up for the narrator's disappointment, Elstir offers him a sketch of the *Port de Carquethuit*. The narrator says that he would like a photograph of the picture of the young women in masculine costume. Suddenly he realizes that the picture is a portrait of Mme Swann before her marriage and that Elstir is the vulgar, immoral M. Biche of the Verdurin circle. Elstir sees what he is thinking and is generous enough to explain to him that the mistakes we make are fruitful, and that people who never make mistakes never grow. This act illustrates his present generous nature, for he is more concerned with instructing the narrator than with defending himself.

The next few days are taken up by Saint-Loup's preparations for joining his unit at Doncières, since he is a junior officer. The narrator's grandmother makes him a parting present of some letters of Proudhon. Saint-Loup's pleasure at this gift is touching in its candor and ingenuousness. It is obvious that his is a truly noble soul, and that his nobility does not derive merely from his lineage. The narrator is fortunate to have such a friend, who begs the narrator, when he comes to see him off at the station, to visit him at Doncières. As it happens, Bloch, who has a real gift for being where he is not wanted, is hanging around, and Saint-Loup feels he cannot exclude him from the invitation. In consequence, wild horses could not keep Bloch from going to Doncières at the earliest opportunity, whereas the narrator puts off going indefinitely, not because of the presence of Bloch but in order to pursue the *petite bande*, and particularly Albertine Simonet.

He persuades Elstir to invite him to a tea party together with this young lady, and to his utter astonishment he actually meets a true young lady, for he had expected someone wild and unconventional. Albertine is famous among Proustians for her elusiveness. Later, this elusiveness will take other forms, but for the moment it consists of Albertine's talent for seeming different every time the narrator meets her. For the moment, he is disappointed, but decides that he will use her as an intermediary to meet the other members of the *petite bande*. The next few times he sees her she has a rough way of speaking that is not at all ladylike, and she seems interested in keeping him to herself. However, in a few days he has got to know all the members of the *petite bande* and has even contemplated running off with another member, Gisèle. He flits from Gisèle to Andrée to Albertine to Rosemonde like an amorous butterfly in a bower of roses.

Meanwhile, the narrator is completely neglecting Saint-Loup. The Marquise de Villeparisis seems to have vanished from the face of the earth. But because the members of the *petite bande* are friends of Elstir, the narrator does drop in on him from time to time. Elstir, knowing the girls' tastes, shows them pictures of horse races and regattas reminiscent of Degas, Manet, and Renoir. He also likes to discuss suitable clothes with them. Albertine is inspired to express a wish for a yacht and a car. In time the narrator will actually offer her a yacht and a car, but with the irony of fate, these offers will be funereal ones. There is a great contrast between the sunny happiness of the narrator's first visit to Balbec and the tragedy of his later love. For the time being, the narrator, devoid as usual of premonitions, simply wishes to see in reality everything Elstir has painted, just as he had once wanted to visit the places described in books. He fails to realize that it is the artist's vision that gives his works their value.

When they want to have fun in a less artistic way, the narrator and the *petite bande* go up on the cliff to picnic and play very childish games. The narrator enjoys these activities so much that he even writes to Saint-Loup to tell him not to come for a visit because he is involved in urgent family affairs. In reality the family affairs are not what he hopes Saint-Loup thinks. The narrator goes even further, and says that he profits far more from the egotistical pleasures of love (which is what Proust calls them) than from friendship, which prevents him from delving into himself. And he is happy to hear these girls discussing a topic for the *baccalauréat* in a way in which he would be not happy to hear Saint-Loup discoursing on Proudhon.

But this bower of roses is not without its thorns. Albertine, who had written him a declaration of love at one moment, gets angry with him when he makes her lose in a game of *furet* because he wants to hold her hand, and says she does not want to play with him any more. To console him, Andrée, who seems interested in him too, leads him before a hedge of those very hawthorns that had been his first love in Combray, and he is reminded of the past, but not for long. It will be a long time yet he truly learns to respond to these little signs of his true destiny. For a while he makes use of Andrée's continued attentions, but he annoys her by the way he continues to think of Albertine.

Albertine gets over her annoyance with the narrator and invites him to join her in her room at the Grand Hotel, after she has gone to bed. Quite naturally, the narrator thinks that his chance has come. Once in her room, he bounds toward her to kiss her. She astonishes him by ringing the bell. Albertine the elusive has shown yet another unexpected side of her character. However, she is so attractive that she is used to men making advances to her, and so she does not say anything to anybody about his behavior. And Proust follows this up by telling us at length about Albertine's skill at pleasing as many people as possible, a skill which is necessary to her, since she is poor.

The narrator now believes that his girlfriends are all respectable young ladies. He is quite unaware that, in telling Albertine that he despises lesbians, he has set up a communications barrier between them—a barrier that will cause endless complications later on. At this point in his evolution, he feels brotherly toward her, a feeling that will bind him closer to her when they meet again. All that remains is to leave Balbec and the sun, which remains like a mummy of itself now that the season is over.

Chapter Four
Le Côté de Guermantes (The Guermantes Way)

Part 1

If one reads straight on from *A l'ombre des jeunes filles en fleurs* one suffers a slight shock when reading the first sentence of *Le Côté de Guermantes*: "Le pépiement des oiseaux semblait insipide à Françoise" (Françoise considered the twittering of the birds insipid).[1] We have heard about Françose as a cook, a nursemaid, and a general domestic, even as a seamstress, but that she should have a critical attitude to birdsong comes as a surprise. In the second sentence, the narrator explains that the family has moved to an apartment attached to the Hôtel de Guermantes, so that the grandmother, who is not well, can breathe a purer air, and that both he and Françoise are having difficulty making an adjustment to their new home.

We hear nothing about the trip back from Balbec or the adjustment the narrator has had to make to being back in Paris again. We are up against one of the blanks in Proust's narrative that indicate that the narrator is simply not giving any thought to someone or something. We see what he meant when he talked about Mme de Sévigné describing things as they appear to us. When the narrator forgets Balbec, he does not say "I had temporarily forgotten Balbec." He simply does not mention it. Now he is preoccupied by being in the vicinity of the Hôtel de Guermantes.

We recognize in the title of these two volumes one of the "ways" along which the narrator went for walks in Combray. We have already been along Swann's way, which seems to be the way of what Proust calls love, and now, with the Guermantes way, we are venturing into the domain of the French aristocracy, with which the narrator conducts a love affair of a different sort. He had not been particularly enamoured of the aristocratic lineage of Robert de Saint-Loup, but his infatuation with the Duchesse de Guermantes makes him long to be accepted by her aristocratic circle.

Proust indignantly protested to his contemporaries that his narrator was not a snob, but you have to understand this protest in a rather special sense to believe him. Certainly, the narrator is not seeking any material advantage by wishing to cultivate the acquaintance of the Duchesse de Guermantes. He is in love with the artistic and historical associations of her name, with all the power of his imagination. The narrator's state of mind is perhaps not unlike that of someone who has a rendezvous in Sherwood Forest to meet a descendant of Robin Hood.

For the moment, the narrator attributes much of his fascination with the Hôtel de Guermantes to Françoise, who has established friendly relations with another tenant, Jupien, the waistcoat maker whom the narrator's grandmother had considered more distinguished than the Duc de Guermantes. Jupien and his niece will have considerable importance in the volumes that follow *Le Côté de Guermantes*—they are two more *personnages préparés*. But Françoise, the shrewd peasant, takes a very factual interest in the Hôtel de Guermantes, whereas her young master is quite unable to keep his imagination on the leash. The Duc seems friendly enough, in a casual way that masks his pride, but the narrator doubts that this will make it easier for him to get to know the Duchesse and grasp the fantastic reality that her name suggests.

Since there is a functionary in the offices of Fate whose task it is to grant the narrator's wishes, with all the irony that such grants imply, the narrator is presented with a ticket to the Opéra to see Berma in one act of *Phèdre*, on a night when the Duchesse de Guermantes will also be there. Since it is a gala evening, the Opéra is full of aristocrats. The narrator sees all these nobles in their boxes as so many demigods. Partly because he is so preoccupied by their splendor, he is able to listen to Berma in a relaxed frame of mind, without the nervous tension that had characterized his first attempt to appreciate her. Now he realizes for the first time that she is a great actress because she does not *act* her parts, she *becomes* them. Furthermore, she is just as great an actress in a play inferior to the masterpiece *Phèdre*. She is a true creator, in the same sense as Elstir, for whom the intrinsic beauty of the things he paints makes very little difference. However, the narrator has no desire to see Berma again, because he is completely satisfied. His imagination has not come between himself and Berma to make him hope for greater heights on another occasion. It is otherwise occupied—that is, with the Duchesse de Guermantes, who arrives in the box of her cousin, the Princesse de Guermantes, halfway through the performance, thus demonstrating her and her cousin's complete indifference to Berma.

Both the Duchesse and the Princesse are beautiful and marvelously dressed. The narrator finds it impossible to think that any other women could wear their clothes, which seem to him like the unchangeable attributes of goddesses. Just as he is gazing at these goddesses, the Duchesse de Guermantes waves and smiles at him. She has actually recognized *him* in the anonymous crowd of the orchestra. We hear nothing more of the remainder of the evening, which is blotted out by the dazzling favor the narrator has received. He moves on to tell us that every morning from then on he took up his position in the streets where the Duchesse took her walks, in order to be able to exchange greetings with her. Not that this devotion does him much good, because the Duchesse is thoroughly annoyed at having her footsteps dogged by this young man, and is in no mood to repeat the dazzling smile that she bestowed on him at the Opéra.

The narrator exhibits one of the less familiar features of Proustian love in that he is unable to remember from one day to the next what the Duchesse looks like. This inability to remember the beloved's features is a sign that she has been so deeply absorbed into the narrator's imagination that there is no room left for her as a person. As for his pursuit of her, obviously it is completely egocentric. No Proustian lover really cares at all for his beloved's feelings. The wish to spare her annoyance or even more negative feelings simply does not enter the Proustian lover's mind. Quite the opposite. The desire to possess and contain, which we noticed in the passages on reading in "Combray," seems to be what characterizes the Proustian lover's kind of love. But the narrator cannot read the Duchesse like a book, although he would like to.

Someone who can read *him* like a book is Françoise, whose feelings about him are so different from what he thinks that he doubts whether we can ever know the truth, even about those we love. Here he has a fleeting premonition of what he is to go through later over Albertine. Françoise's opinion of him is that he is out of his mind—and maybe he is. The narrator acknowledges that he is *nerveux* (high-strung) and consequently liable to behave in a bizarre way, but the emotion he calls "love" seems to unsettle him even more.

Suddenly he has a bright idea: he will visit Robert de Saint-Loup whose friendship leaves him basically indifferent, and get him to speak highly of him to the Duchesse de Guermantes, who is Saint-Loup's aunt. No sooner thought than done: he arrives at Doncières and goes straight to Saint-Loup's quarters. Imagining that the narrator has come to see him out of affection, an illusion the narrator is careful not to dispel, Saint-

Loup sets about finding a hotel for the narrator that will not distress him too much. Saint-Loup is full of tender, loving concern for the narrator, in a way that the latter simply does not deserve. He even arranges for the narrator to spend the first night in his own room, since Saint-Loup is not free to accompany the narrator to the hotel. The narrator is moved to tears by this kindness, even though at the same time he is plotting to get Saint-Loup to give him a photograph of the Duchesse.

The narrator is deeply intrigued by Saint-Loup's captain, the Prince de Borodino, a member of the imperial nobility, whose aristocratic status is disdained by members of the older, pre-Napoleonic nobility. Earlier, in "Un Amour de Swann," the Duchesse de Guermantes had sneered at the Jénas because they too were imperial nobles. He also takes pleasure in recognizing the Duchesse's features in the face of Saint-Loup. He sees something mythological in these features—the results of the union of a goddess with a bird. Even Saint-Loup, whose friendship he takes so much for granted, appears superhuman because of the family resemblance.

The narrator leaves the barracks to spend his second night at Doncières in a charming hotel that is a converted château. He is so delighted by this hotel that he has no difficulty sleeping in it. The narrator's preoccupation with the Duchesse de Guermantes seems to be giving way a little to other impressions. One of these is his constant reliance on Saint-Loup to solve all his problems. Another is his growing interest in military life. The wish to penetrate into a way of life unknown to him, which he had earlier thought he could achieve by making love to girls and women, is actually being granted in a masculine atmosphere without making love to anyone. Perhaps he should deduce from this that he would do better to leave women alone, but he does not reach this conclusion. He is simply aware that he is happy, and not only happy, but more healthy than usual. And, for quite different reasons than Swann at the soirée of Mme de Saint-Euverte, everything and everyone he sees around him seems like some element in a series of great paintings.

In the midst of all these pleasures the narrator suddenly remembers the Duchesse de Guermantes and asks three favors of Saint-Loup. One is to praise him to her. The second is to get her to ask him to dinner. And the third is for Saint-Loup to give him her photograph. Saint-Loup is quite willing to accord the first two, but balks at the third. However, he does not bear a grudge against the narrator, but acts as his cheerleader in a conversation involving his friends and the narrator in the restaurant where the narrator has just made these requests.

The conversation turns on the Dreyfus affair, which will run through

Le Côté de Guermantes, part 1, like a leitmotif. Although Proust himself was passionately interested in the fate of Dreyfus, the Jewish captain falsely accused of treason, the narrator expresses no personal opinion on the affair, but is inclined to take a rather malicious pleasure in reporting the various opinions of people on either side, while indicating how little factual basis they have. There is even a suggestion at this point that these discussions do not rise above the level of ordinary gossip. Proust's humor can be cruel, but the cutting edge is frequently directed against himself and what he really cares about. And although Saint-Loup is on the side of Dreyfus, we do not hear his reasons for this belief at the moment, but only about his emotional commitment. What interests the narrator far more is Saint-Loup's exposition of strategy as a fine art.

In the midst of this conversation comes another of those little paradoxical suggestions that Saint-Loup, though he may appear to be homosexual, cannot possibly be so (his first appearance at Balbec included a similar hint). Modern criticism often assumes that he is and was homosexual from the start, but a literal reading of Proust indicates that Saint-Loup's later conversion to homosexuality is part of a genetic evolution. Is the narrator naive, or is he disingenuous, or are we to take Proust at his word? It is often hard to tell.

At the moment, however, it is certain that Robert de Saint-Loup is in love with a woman who surfaces very shortly. He is suffering because he and his mistress have had a quarrel and he has no idea what her silence means. But his imagination and his jealousy provide him with plenty of ideas of what she may be doing. According to the iron law of Proustian love, he loves her more than she loves him, and therefore must suffer. We have seen the same situation with Swann and Odette, we are seeing it now with Robert de Saint-Loup and his mistress, and we will see it again, magnified, with the narrator and Albertine. Proust never shows us anyone who is happy in love. Married couples are different, because they are not in love. Luckily the narrator's infatuation with the Duchesse de Guermantes is too one-sided to bring him more than a little suffering, which will soon be over.

A reconciliation between Saint-Loup and his mistress is effected, but only after he agrees to put off going to Paris. The presence of Saint-Loup in Paris means just one thing to the narrator: access to the Duchesse de Guermantes, whom he now claims he wants to visit in order to see her collection of paintings by Elstir. There is a grain of truth in this claim because the narrator really does want to see more paintings by Elstir, but all the same, the Elstirs provide him with an excuse to visit her even without Saint-Loup's company. His friend agrees to arrange this visit.

The account of life at Doncières is interrupted by a telephone call from the narrator's grandmother. Hearing her voice in isolation from everything else about her incites a rush of tenderness and pity in the narrator. Since love of family is the only kind of love that Proust is willing to endorse, it is with the full approval of everyone that the narrator gets ready to go back to Paris, to be with his grandmother. But before he leaves, he is summoned to the telephone a second time, to talk with somebody else's grandmother, by way of a little light relief. When the narrator arrives in Paris and sees his grandmother, he suddenly sees how old and confused she has become. The sound of her voice was the first premonition of her death, and this sight of her is the second.

However, the narrator does not dwell on this painful discovery, and is soon at his old activity of pursuing the Duchesse de Guermantes, who has no intention of inviting him to see her Elstirs. But M. de Norpois encourages the narrator, through his father, to go and visit the Marquise de Villeparisis. At the same time, the Dreyfus case suddenly impinges on the family, when their old neighbor from Combray, Mme Sazerat, greets the narrator's father very coldly because he is against Dreyfus and she is for him. It is not only military circles, but the country as a whole that views the Dreyfus affair as a crucial issue. Indeed, when the narrator finally does pay the Marquise a visit, Dreyfus will be a prominent topic of conversation.

Saint-Loup returns to Paris in the spring, and takes the narrator out with him to the suburbs to meet his mistress, whom he does not know how to praise highly enough, in spite (or because) of the trouble she gives him. Like Swann, he is trying to bind her to him with expensive gifts, in this case a valuable necklace. Also like Swann so long as he was in love, Saint-Loup does not intend to marry her, because he wants her to always have more to wish for. But the narrator is not particularly concerned about Saint-Loup's love affair, for he has eyes only for the pear and cherry trees in bloom that abound in this suburb and which, together with the lilacs, bring back memories of the innocence of Combray. Saint-Loup leaves the narrator gazing at a pear tree and goes to fetch his mistress whom the narrator identifies as Rachel, a cheap prostitute who had earlier been offered to him for 20 francs. There follows a meditation on the difference between the enormous emotional value Saint-Loup places on her and the monetary value of 20 francs, a number that recurs with deadly scorn. The contrast is emblemized by the narrator's view of the

village, which looks as if it had been burned by fire from heaven, and a
dazzlingly white pear tree, which looks like an angel.

Two of Rachel's cheap, vulgar girlfriends greet her as they are about to
get on the train to Paris, and Saint-Loup for a moment sees her as a person
like them, but this moment of recognition quickly passes. They are all
soon in a restaurant where Rachel talks literature, scolds her lover for
drinking wine, and quarrels with him, which is a frequent occurrence
because Saint-Loup, like Swann, is jealous of every man she looks at. She
is different from Odette, however, because she is an actress who takes her
art very seriously and has real claims to taste and intelligence. Because of
her Saint-Loup is on the side of Dreyfus, whom she calls a martyr. He is
very impressed by her ideas. The narrator, however, having been informed by Mme de Villeparisis that she has no talent, is not impressed by
Rachel.

One really appreciates how Rachel makes life difficult for Saint-Loup
when we see her driving him wild with jealousy in the restaurant,
insulting him over the valuable necklace he had intended to give her,
organizing her friends to boo a singer off the stage, and making passes
before Saint-Loup's eyes at a male dancer in women's clothes. She
torments him, and anyone else who displeases her, as much as she
possibly can. Since Saint-Loup is too much of a gentleman to beat her,
he deals with his anger by slapping a journalist who refuses to put out his
cigar and then by thrashing a homosexual who accosts him in the street.
No doubt feeling better after this, he leaves the narrator to go on alone to
see Mme de Villeparisis. In consequence, putting all this wild behavior
out of his mind, the narrator proceeds to reflect on Mme de Villeparisis.

He has no difficulty realizing that M. de Norpois is Mme de Villeparisis's lover, but he does not consider this liaison enough to account for
the lack of prestige of her salon, whose members seem limited mostly to
family. He is inclined to suppose that she has just a little too much talent
to suit the nobility. However, that talent will make her salon seem
brilliant later on when she publishes her memoirs.

The description of Mme de Villeparisis's salon, from the moment the
narrator arrives to the moment he leaves, takes up over 100 pages in
the Flammarion edition and consists chiefly of conversations between the
various people who enter, none of whom says anything of apparent
intrinsic value. This section may sound very dull, but in fact it is
extremely comic, partly because of the fundamental absurdity of the
characters' remarks, and partly because of the bizarre expressions many of
them use. Proust reveals the sheer emptiness of high society as each

stupid and annoying aristocrat enters and reveals his or her foibles. The same applies to the bourgeois guests who seek out this relatively accessible entrance to the haunts of the aristocracy. But the narrator himself will not fully realize that this is what *all* high society is really like until the second part of *Le Côté de Guermantes*, for he is quite aware that the salon of Mme de Villeparisis is third-rate. That the gods and goddesses he saw at the Opéra are only ordinary human beings is a realization that he is not, as yet, prepared to make.

The narrator arrives unfashionably early. He finds the Marquise de Villeparisis just interrupting her painting of flowers in the company of an archivist with whom she has been classifying autograph letters from crowned heads for her memoirs, and a historian who has come to look at her portrait of the Duchesse de Montmorency. The ubiquitous Bloch arrives shortly thereafter, for he is attracting notice as a dramatist and Mme de Villeparisis wants him to entice actors to play before her salon for no pay. The Dreyfus affair is making Jews extremely unwelcome in society, but Mme de Villeparisis keeps out of politics. Presumably she does not want to encroach on the field of M. de Norpois. The narrator, on the other hand, makes some derogatory reflections on the Semitic appearance of his friend. However, he keeps them to himself. It is just as well, for if he had spoken them out loud, he would have sounded almost like the Baron de Charlus. As Compagnon suggests, the narrator, unlike the other characters, is allowed to get away with everything (302).

Bloch, who is not at all shy about expressing what is on his mind, questions Mme de Villeparisis about the habits of the aristocracy, and she is delighted to reply, because it gives her an opportunity to try out parts of her memoirs in advance. The historian tries to join in, but no one pays any attention to him. The historian's role in this episode is curiously reminiscent of the role of Saniette in the Verdurin circle episodes. These circles are not so different as the people who compose them think.

Next to enter is an old lady, known as Alix, who is one of three aristocratic ladies who created so much scandal in the Faubourg Saint-Germain in their youth that they have been dropped to the very bottom of the aristocratic social ladder. Mme de Villeparisis herself is, of course, in the same position, and the two women try to score little advantages over one another. But each of them has a niece with a brilliant social position who will not abandon them, because they are related.

The Duchesse de Guermantes, Mme de Villeparisis's brilliant niece, comes in. Hard on her heels is Legrandin, who has tried again and again to enter this salon, while continuing to claim that he despises snobs. He is extremely disconcerted to find the narrator present, as a witness to his hypocrisy. Standing at a distance from the narrator in the hope that he will not hear, Legrandin proceeds to heap one flattery after another on Mme de Villeparisis.

The Duchesse de Guermantes asks who Legrandin is and then exclaims that she has been forced to receive his sister, Mme de Cambremer. She is extremely rude about both Legrandin and his sister. In spite of her lack of manners, she excites wonder and admiration in the narrator.

A writer called G. comes in and immediately seeks out the Duchesse as an old acquaintance. He is one of many prominent intellectuals whom the Duchesse invites, but not so as to have intellectual conversations. The Duchesse's intelligence consists chiefly of making outrageous remarks that pass for wit and of having a high opinion of Bergotte. The narrator is distressed to think that if he had not avoided Bergotte on his first visit to the Opéra he could have made the acquaintance of the Duchesse back then.

The Comte d'Argencourt, the Baron de Guermantes, and the Duc de Châtellerault enter next. But in this little comedy they are not of the first importance.

Bloch calls attention to himself for a moment by knocking over Mme de Villeparisis's vase of flowers, and then by noting that the accident did not matter because he had not got wet. He goes on to give other examples of his complete lack of manners. He proposes, for instance, to bring Rachel to recite before Mme de Villeparisis, a great blunder, for all Saint-Loup's relatives are violently opposed to his affair with her. Before he can make any more gaffes, the Marquise de Villeparisis sends a servant to fetch the Marquis de Norpois so that Bloch can talk to him about the Dreyfus affair. This conversation is a real Proustian gem because Bloch persistently attempts to discover the old ambassador's position on the affair, while the Marquis uses all his diplomatic skill to conceal it. Meanwhile, the Marquis de Norpois seizes the opportunity to snub the narrator for his admiration for Bergotte and Elstir.

The Duc de Guermantes comes in, without interrupting the conversation between the narrator and the Marquis de Norpois. The narrator asks the Marquis de Norpois to vote for his father in the forthcoming election to the Académie des Sciences Morales. To his surprise, M. de Norpois refuses. The Duchesse de Guermantes runs down Rachel, who had recited some Maeterlinck at her house, and Mme de Villeparisis's other guests run down Maeterlinck as well, to the disgust of the narrator. Then the Duchesse, with the encouragement of her husband, who does not love her but is proud of her wit, adds to her denigration of Mme de Cambremer. Then they get back to Rachel, followed by discussion of the Jews and the Dreyfus affair. Anti-Semitism is characteristic of this social circle, and the visitors, even the Duc de Châtellerault, who is secretly pro-Dreyfus, all band together to hound Bloch out of the room. Since Bloch is persistently ridiculous, his main reaction is one of astonishment that anyone should recognize him as Jewish.

The Vicomtesse de Marsantes, Robert de Saint-Loup's mother, enters, and the Jewish subject is dropped. However, Mme de Marsantes takes it up again, being both violently anti-Dreyfus and anti-Semitic presumably because of her son's affair with Rachel. But then Saint-Loup comes in, and his mother is overcome with joy. Saint-Loup tries to get the narrator together with the Duchesse de Guermantes, which she does not much appreciate.

The Prince von Faffenheim-Munsterburg-Weinigen (Prince Von) arrives to pay homage to the Marquise de Villeparisis, hoping by this action to get M. de Norpois to vote for him at the Académie des Sciences Morales. He is closely followed by Mme Swann, at whose sight the Duchesse leaves, for she has always refused to have anything to do with Mme Swann. Mme Swann has been making her way in society by being anti-Dreyfus, although the narrator remembers her saying in the past that she was sure Dreyfus was innocent. Mme Swann is immediately joined by M. de Charlus. They are old friends, and in any case M. de Charlus always makes a great show of paying court to any attractive woman in a gathering. However, he is much more interested in the narrator than in Mme Swann.

Mme de Villeparisis, who is aware of the Baron de Charlus's homosexual proclivities, tries to prevent the narrator from going off with him, but the Baron catches up with him and makes mysterious proposals to him, one being that he get Bloch to combat his father, as David did Goliath, and beat his mother. Charlus is anti-Semitic to the point of considering Jews as foreigners, and less than human to boot. Naturally, he is against Dreyfus. But these grotesque remarks are nothing next to his suggestion that he can arrange a brilliant political career for the narrator. What he actually has in mind is that he will initiate him to the world of homosexuality. Then the Baron takes off in search of easier prey. The narrator, of course, has no idea what to make of all this. Nor at this time does the Baron have any idea that the great love of his life will not be the narrator, but Charles Morel, the son of Uncle Adolphe's valet, who aspires to a musical career. We learn of Charles Morel's ambition from the narrator in the course of his visit to the Marquise de Villeparisis, when he also informs us that "the lady in pink" he had surprised with his Uncle Adolphe was Mme Swann. As the saying goes, anything can happen and usually does.

The narrator goes home to find his family's butler discussing the Dreyfus case with the Guermanteses' butler. But this discovery does not detain him long. He goes inside and finds his grandmother unwell. Cottard is called and prescribes milk dishes, but is unaware of the danger of adding salt. Her temperature is high, so the family tries quinine, but this is simply a case of treating the symptom rather than the illness. Since Cottard's treatment does not work, the family calls in Dr. du Boulbon, a neurologist and psychiatrist recommended by Bergotte. Nor too surprisingly, he assumes that her malady is nervous and urges her to take the air in the Champs-Elysées. A letter from Saint-Loup accusing the narrator of treachery toward him arrives in the midst of the family's relief. The narrator makes no comment on this, as they are all absorbed in getting his grandmother to the Champs-Elysées. Once there, the grandmother has an attack in a public convenience which, in an heroic attempt to deny the cruelty of fate, the grandmother presents under a comic aspect as an exclusive salon, and the narrator has to abandon his plan of leaving his grandmother in the Champs-Elysées while he goes off to enjoy himself. She makes an effort to reassure him with a couple of her favorite quotations, but this effort merely underlines her state of near-collapse.

Part 2, Chapter 1

To suit his publishers rather than himself, Proust used the final illness and death of the grandmother as a hinge between the two volumes of *Le Côté de Guermantes*, expressing fully the suffering that lies behind the narrator's comic verve. Proust's irony has a cutting edge that is turned against himself quite as much as against other people, and this first chapter, which is entirely devoted to the grandmother's death agony, described in cruel detail, with all of Dr. Cottard's hopeless efforts to save her, is scattered with humorous effects.

Professor E., to whom the narrator had turned while still on the way home with his grandmother, is more preoccupied with the grand dinner he is soon to attend than with the condition of the narrator's grandmother, whom he pronounces beyond saving. Françoise, in her mixture of devotion and callousness, makes the distress of the grandmother and her family harder to bear. Bergotte pays the family lengthy visits, more because he has nowhere else to go that suits him than out of commiseration with the family. The grandmother's sisters decide that they will grieve for her more effectively by listening to Beethoven than by coming to her bedside. The Duc de Guermantes turns up at the moment of the death agony, convinced that he is doing the family a favor and offended because the narrator's mother does not appreciate his compliments. At the same time he is delighted to run into Saint-Loup in their apartment, and keeps repeating how lucky he is. A monk, the grandmother's brother-in-law, pretends to pray at the grandmother's bedside in order to spy on the narrator's grief. And a cousin who has the habit of going to funerals turns up, quite in his element. The Molièresque nature of these characters and of the whole situation, which has been underlined by Roger Shattuck,[2] is accentuated by the name of the real doctor who comes to confirm the death, M. Dieulafoy. Proust only leaves off tormenting his readers and himself by saying that once the grandmother is dead, she looks like a young girl.

Part 2, Chapter 2

We find the narrator in bed on an autumn day, gazing at the mist, which reminds him of Doncières, and listening to the hiccups of the central heating that will become associated with Doncières in his mind. He is waiting for a letter from Mme de Stermaria to whom Saint-Loup assures him that he has a good chance of making love. He also intends to see a little dramatic sketch at the home of the Marquise de Villeparisis, while fully aware that this plan is not entirely consistent with his official mourning. Otherwise, his grandmother is not at all on his mind. His parents are in Combray, so he is free to do as he likes.

Albertine comes to pay him a visit, and her vocabulary has changed so much that he concludes that she has changed too. He takes advantage of this supposed change to kiss her—on the cheek—while commenting to himself on the unsatisfactory nature of kissing. They are interrupted by Françoise, bearing a lamp, like Justice revealing Crime, and after that proceed to a conclusion that the narrator compares to his orgasm while wrestling with Gilberte. This comparison suggests that actual penetration does not take place.

After Albertine leaves, expressing her willingness to return at any time, the narrator receives a letter from Mme de Stermaria accepting his invitation to dinner in the Bois de Boulogne. The narrator is overjoyed, for he believes that what he feels for Mme de Stermaria, unlike what he feels for Albertine, is love. That is to say that the former has excited his imagination, which is no longer the case with the latter.

He arrives late at the home of Mme de Villeparisis, after the theatrical sketch is over, and meets the Duchesse de Guermantes, with whom he is no longer in love because his mother had persuaded him to stop following her about. Consequently, since his attitude toward the Duchesse de Guermantes has become normal, she has taken a liking to him. It is one of Proust's maxims that you always get what you want once you have stopped wanting it, and this applies particularly to love, because we are attracted by the people who show that they can do without us, not only in love but in all social relations. This seems to be something Proust himself really believed, and is not just one of the quirks he attributes to the narrator. Consequently, in conformity with this logic, the Duchesse de Guermantes invites the narrator to dinner—and not just to any dinner, but to a grand one, with the Princesse de Parme as the principal guest.

He accepts, for a day convenient for him, but what is on his mind at this moment is his dinner with Mme de Stermaria. He is so preoccupied with her and has so little thought of Albertine that he takes the latter with him to the Bois de Boulogne to order a dinner for the former. He is overcome with grief when Mme de Stermaria cancels at the last minute and leaves him, alone in his parents' apartment, weeping into a rolled-up carpet. From this desolation Saint-Loup comes to rescue him, but his friend's action does not prevent the narrator from thinking disparaging thoughts about the value of friendship, particularly as he has some ideas about Combray, Doncières, and Rivebelle that he would have been free to write down if he had been alone. Consequently, he thinks, he could have begun his writing career years earlier than he did.

They go through the fog to a restaurant that has a clientèle of penurious young aristocrats hoping to make rich marriages, even if they are secretly—or perhaps unwittingly—homosexual. Again, we get a little hint about Saint-Loup. On the way, Saint-Loup reveals that he has told Bloch that the narrator does not like Bloch all that much, but once in the restaurant he exudes affectionate concern and runs gracefully over the tops of the wall-sofas to bring him the Prince de Foix's vicuna coat, to keep the narrator warm without disturbing him. He also has an important message for the narrator: he is to pay a visit to the Baron de Charlus at 11:00 P.M., after the Guermantes dinner party.

The Baron de Charlus puzzles the narrator more and more. After eyeing Bloch in the street, he was furious when the narrator attempted to

introduce them, and he has been claiming to the Duchesse de Guermantes that he has never met the narrator and would like to meet him. Now
it is particularly important that the narrator come to see him, so late in
the evening. But the narrator is no longer surprised, because the Duchesse de Guermantes has given him the idea that the Baron de Charlus is
half crazy. Consequently, he is not particularly concerned about the
Baron's wish to see him, and meditates instead about the manners of the
aristocracy.

The restaurant scene fades into the Hôtel de Guermantes, where the
normally vulgar Duc shows the narrator his manners at their best. The
Duc de Guermantes, when he is not even thinking of being polite, is so
marked by the manners of an older time, that he arouses a historical
interest in the narrator. But before pursuing this historical interest, for
the time being, the narrator satisfies an artistic one by taking a look at the
Guermantes Elstir paintings. He had once used a wish to see the
Duchesse's Elstirs as a pretext for getting close to her; now the Elstirs
hold his attention much more than the Duchesse herself does.

This is one of the ways by which Proust demonstrates the changes
brought about by the passage of time. We have already seen times's
passages clearly illustrated in his attitude toward Albertine. The French
say "Il ne faut jamais dire; fontaine, je ne boirai pas de ton eau" (You
should never say of anything that it would never happen to you). Yet
there is good reason for the narrator to retain his admiration for Elstir in
the midst of his passing loves. The human need to fall in love remains,
but the objects of this love vary. Hence the narrator's remark that if Mme
de Stermaria had kept her appointment, he might have had a great love
affair with her. But because she broke her appointment the opportunity
for such an affair was lost. Women are interchangeable, but Elstir is not
interchangeable with another artist, any more than Berma is interchangeable with another actress. Art is the supreme value in a way in
which love is not. Love is a passing fancy, created by the imagination of
the lover, but art endures. Even if there comes a time when Bergotte will
become easy to read, his books are the truest and most permanent part of
him. And this is just as true of the paintings of Elstir.

The description of the Guermantes Elstirs does not last very long, but
the narrator loses all sense of time looking at them. As I have already
noted, the Elstir of Balbec had been quite definitely an impressionist in
the style of Manet, Monet, and Degas, with his regattas and races and
views of rocks jutting out into the sea, when he was not like Turner in his
tricks of perspective. What chiefly characterizes most of the Elstirs in

this episode seems to be the style of Renoir, particularly that of *Le Moulin de la Galette* and *Luncheon Boating Party*, which Proust seems to have fused together. There also remains a touch of Monet in that Elstir paints both a cathedral and a hospital in the same way, making them equally glorious. Moreover, in the course of the Guermanteses' dinner party, the narrator will compare two of the Guermantes Elstirs to Manet. Elstir is mainly an amalgam of all the impressionists, in spite of the fact that his early manner is that of Gustave Moreau. Still, this is not incredible. Picasso, for instance, had a great many manners, very different from each other.

What strikes the narrator more than anything else is the idiosyncratic nature of Elstir's vision, of which his conversation gives no idea. As the narrator will insist in *Le Temps retrouvé*, the work of art has supreme value because it is only through the work of art that the personal vision of the creator is expressed, enabling us to see through the eyes of others, something that we could never do otherwise. We grasp nothing of other people's real values through conversation, a principle that Proust really rubs in by taking his readers with the narrator from his contemplation of the Elstirs to the inane conversation of the Guermanteses' dinner party.

However, we must wait to hear this conversation. After the narrator comes to himself, having held up the dinner party for nearly an hour, and being treated with the utmost politeness in spite of the delay he has caused, the Duc de Guermantes hastens to introduce him to the Princesse de Parme. We are now treated to a lengthy disquisition on the Princesse de Parme, the Guermanteses, their cousins the Courvoisiers, and the aristocratic guests in general that extends for nearly 80 pages. Adopting a poker face to talk about the frothy trifles of which aristocratic life is composed, writing as seriously about aristocratic frivolity as if he were a paleontologist reconstructing a dinosaur, Proust dissects the Guermanteses and their dinner party before we sit down to it.

Of the world, the flesh, and the devil, Proust is best disposed toward the flesh, even though his narrator is too sickly to be able to indulge in it very much, and the passages he considered "obscene" lack the direct physical description that we find, for instance, in Henry Miller. This is because of Proust's reverence for the creative arts. The flesh can be helpful to a creative artist because it makes him go deeply into himself, but what characterizes the world is its insistence on remaining on the surface and making manners a substitute for real qualities. As for the devil, Proust never mentions him by name, but he seems to be present whenever someone is indifferent to suffering or actively cruel.

Satire takes wing with Proust's introduction of the Princesse de Parme, who is extremely humble because she is extremely proud of her noble birth and her enormous wealth. She has been taught since childhood to be modest and kind to her social inferiors, by way of showing her gratitude to God, but also to avoid inviting such inferiors to her salon because that would diminish its value. Her amiable manner is also typical of the "flower maidens" with whom the narrator, as a new Parsifal, finds himself surrounded, and who are actually society ladies dressed in deep décolleté. Saying nice things costs nothing, and does not entail the necessity to live up to them.

M. Hannibal de Bréauté-Consalvi is just as keen to get to know the narrator as the women are. Since he knows the narrator does not belong to "Society," he supposes that the narrator must be some celebrity, for the Guermanteses are in the habit of inviting from time to time some man who has done something notable—but not too often, because an overdose of bourgeois would ruin the standing of their salon. The narrator compares the smiles M. de Bréauté rains on him with the attitude of an explorer in the presence of some savage tribe while exchanging pieces of glass for ostrich eggs and spices.

But the narrator does give credit where credit is due in appreciating the historic interest of the aristocratic manners of the Duc de Guermantes. From there he takes off on a detailed study of the physical and moral characteristics of the Guermanteses, who dare to break with the conventions of high society, and yet do not go so far as to put themselves beyond the pale. He contrasts them with the Courvoisiers, who are as well born and as rich, but much more conventional, much as one might contrast a zebra with a pony. But underneath this comparison is the implicit judgment that the originality and independence that make the Duchesse de Guermantes, in particular, so much admired by the Princesse de Parme do not go much beneath the surface. The prejudices of the Courvoisiers are just as strong in the Duchesse de Guermantes. She simply contents herself with refusing to pay them lip-service, to the exasperation of the Courvoisiers.

When the banquet actually begins, we see the Duchesse de Guermantes in action, delighting the Princess de Parme with her paradoxes, which are frequently direct untruths and equally frequently extremely unkind. The much-admired Duchesse, embittered by her husband's neglect, not only enjoys making her husband's cast-off mistress, Mme d'Arpajon, feel small, which is only natural, but also deliberately destroys the happiness of her servant, Poullein, who was looking forward to his day off to see his fiancée. The Duchesse de Guermantes makes him change days with another servant. She is revealed to be cold, petty, and malicious. But the Princesse de Parme, under the spell of her charm, does not see this truth.

We get a little whiff of brimstone, as we move toward *Sodome et Gomorrhe*, when the Duchesse starts saying that the Baron de Charlus mourns his wife as if she were anything but a wife, and so makes the Duc angry with her. There is something a bit suggestive about the way Prince Von tries to get the narrator away from the Baron de Charlus. There is also something suggestive about the way the Duc de Châtellerault smiles at the servant who jogs his elbow. But at no point does Proust suggest that homosexuality is the exclusive preserve of the aristocracy. Rather, he intends to suggest that nothing can suppress it, anywhere.

The time perspective slips a little as we learn that after this dinner party the narrator is invited out a good deal by friends of the Guermanteses and also by the Guermanteses themselves. His intimacy with the Guermanteses reaches the point where he is provided with a jug of cooked cherry or pear juice all to himself, in addition to the ritual Guermantes orangeade which is good enough for everyone else. But then the scene becomes more clear again with the reception at which we hear the Duchesse de Guermantes making all kinds of excuses to avoid asking General de Monserfeuil for the change in posting that Robert de Saint-Loup desires. If Saint-Loup dies at his post, the Duchesse thinks, that would be better than enabling him to get together with Rachel.

The Princesse de Parme, alarmed at the rude remarks the Duchesse de Guermantes is making about General de Monserfeuil, changes the conversation to some flowers in a pot, which the Duchesse would like to see pollinated by an insect. These flowers will play an unexpected role later on. For the meantime, the Duchesse talks about the botanical lessons she has learned from Swann and says that she had to give up seeing Swann after his marriage to Odette, a statement that later on is revealed to be not quite true.

From there the Duchesse branches off onto a disquisition on Empire furniture, which she claims to have admired from the start. This is a direct lie, as we know from her conversation at the soirée of Mme de Saint-Euverte, in "Un Amour de Swann," but no one contradicts her. At the same time, the Jénas, whom she refused to go near in "Un Amour de Swann," now are revealed to be apparent friends. She even tries to get the Princesse de Parme to go and visit them with her, which is rather naughty of her, because the Princesse de Parme strongly disapproves of the Jénas, who have taken over a title that actually belongs to her son.

While the Duchesse is about it, she teases the Princesse de Parme a bit farther by talking to her about *Le jeune homme et la mort* by Gustave Moreau, a painting of which the Princesse de Parme is completely ignorant. She repeats the narrator's idea that real innovations in the arts take 40 years for the general public to appreciate and claims to have admired all such innovations, such as Manet's *Olympia*, which now looks like an Ingres, from the start. She goes on to talk about Elstir's portrait of herself and the paintings by Hals in Haarlem, which would be admirable even if one glimpsed them from the top of a streetcar.

Although the Duchesse is at her most dazzling, the narrator is not impressed because she does not truly understand art. However, he is pleased that someone he had supposed to be so different from himself is at least interested in art. Since her guests take their cue from the Duchesse, Prince Von starts talking about the kaiser's complete lack of taste in art, after which he proceeds to talk politics, apparently under the impression that the Duchesse has some influence over the official line of the government, when in fact the Duchesse has no contact with the government whatsoever. All the prestige she recognizes is in the realm of the imaginary, whereas the government is something real, and consequently inferior.

But since the imaginary prestige of the Guermantes and their guests consists of being descended from people who held real power in the past ages, there is a great deal of discussion in the course of the evening about genealogies. For example, there is a discussion about whether a marriage between the Marquis de Norpois and his old mistress, the Marquise de Villeparisis, would be a *mésalliance*. These noble names, redolent of the past and even of Combray, send the narrator off into a dream, giving him his most creative moments of the evening. The Duchesse apologizes for the genealogies, not realizing how valuable they are to him.

However, he is distressed by the unkind and hurtful things these people keep saying about the Grand Duc de Luxembourg, who is apparently a friend of his, although he never notes how they met. Proust's narrative contains a number of these odd blanks. But it is a bit surprising that someone who is on friendly terms with a Grand Duc should not know that he is not supposed to leave before the Princesse de Parme, however eager he may be to join the Baron de Charlus.

In the carriage that now takes him to the home of the Baron de Charlus, he goes over the conversation he has heard. He is in a state of exaltation that is not like that of the times when he has gone deeply into his personal impressions. He is so carried away by the flow of talk by which he has been surrounded that he cannot stop repeating it to himself and longing to repeat it to someone else. In this passage Proust spells out for us, quite specifically, what he had been repeating to us since *Les Plaisirs et les jours*—that a solitary life, with its creative joys, is far preferable to the constant distractions of life in society, which prevent one from entering into contact with oneself.

The narrator arrives at the home of the Baron de Charlus, bursting to tell him everything he has heard at the Guermantes dinner, only to be made to wait indefinitely in an antechamber. A footman arrives and makes excuses—probably lies—for the way the narrator is being made to wait, and eventually the narrator is ushered into the Baron's presence. The Baron is lying down in a Chinese dressing gown, and leaves the narrator standing. Apparently he likes to play the king and leave his guests standing until he chooses to give them permission to sit. But the narrator does not know this, and asks for permission to sit. The Baron tells him to sit in a Louis XIV armchair, and heaps the most amazing and inventive insults on him because he sits in a Directory armchair instead.

He reminds me of Swann cursing the Verdurins for excluding him. Indeed, the Baron's tirades, which get more extraordinary all the time, have the same cause—a disappointment in love. In fact, this idea does occur to the narrator, but only as one of several possibilities. He might have remembered how he would have liked to insult Gilberte, when he was a little boy, when he thought that she had turned him down, but in fact he does not. Soon the Baron is reproaching him for not having been more responsive, and particularly for not having realized that the gift of a book with forget-me-nots stamped on the binding was intended as a request from the Baron not to forget him. Even this intrusion of the sentimental and romantic in the Baron's tirades does not make the narrator realize that the Baron is in love with him and trying by every means in his power to make an indelible impression on him.

Of course, the Baron would never admit that this was the case, so he claims that the narrator had been slandering him—him, the Baron de Charlus, who is so great, so far above the narrator, that the venomous saliva of 500 of his little friends, standing on each other's shoulders, would not reach the Baron's august toes. The narrator is so exasperated by the Baron's insane pride that he falls on the Baron's top hat, tramples it, and tears it to pieces. Then he starts to leave.

This violent act apparently convinces the Baron that he has indeed made an impression, for he pulls the narrator back. Soon, the Baron becomes quite gentle and affectionate with him. He even offers to let him stay the night. Failing that, he has him driven home. On the way to the front door, the Baron points out a painting of a rainbow by Turner that is to be a sign of their reconciliation. At the same time they hear Beethoven's *Pastoral Symphony*, a passage depicting joy after the storm. Quite obviously the Baron has stage-managed the whole thing. He starts stroking the narrator's face, he is so satisfied. And, to make it clear that he wants to see the narrator again, he offers the narrator a special edition of Mme de Sévigné which he is to come and fetch in person. The conversation ends with the Baron's proclamation that no one can enter into contact with the Princesse de Guermantes, who is at the summit of the aristocracy, except through him, and his hint that the narrator would do well to accept his offer of protection.

The narrator, seeing only the Baron's insane pride and readiness to take offence, is quite glad to get away from him. He cheerfully reads a letter that his footman has written on the narrator's stationery and that is full of poetry quotations taken ludicrously out of context. This episode parodies the way poetry was discussed and quoted at the dinner of the Duchesse de Guermantes.

Two months later the narrator receives an invitation to a reception from the Princesse de Guermantes. Even though he had found the Duchesse de Guermantes disappointing, M. de Charlus had made him imagine that the Princesse de Guermantes is so amazing that he cannot be certain that someone has not played a practical joke on him. He would have tried to find out the truth of the matter from the Duc and Duchesse de Guermantes, but they are at Cannes. Then he hears that they have come back, partly because one of their cousins is ill, and partly because the Duc wants to go to a costume ball. The narrator watches for them from the staircase leading to his apartment. What he sees from there is so remarkable that he postpones describing it to the following volume. But he does see the Duc and Duchesse in the courtyard, and goes to visit them.

The Duc de Guermantes receives him, which gives the narrator an opportunity to see certain relatives of the Duc come to tell him that his cousin is close to death. The Duc, determined to go to the costume ball, refuses to take the news seriously. He is annoyed that they are giving up the social events he is so eager to attend because it seems like a slur on him. Finally the narrator asks about his invitation, but the Duc indicates that he has no wish to get involved with the Princesse's invitations.

Although the Duchesse had claimed to have dropped Swann, Swann arrives, in the wake of an enormous photograph of the coins struck by the

Knights of Rhodes, which he had prepared for the Duchesse de Guermantes. She is delighted with the photograph, and invites Swann to
accompany her and the Duc on a trip they plan to take round Italy and
Sicily in a few months. He would be a marvelous artistic guide. Swann
replies that he cannot go on the trip because by that time he will be dead.
(In fact he is reported dead approximately one year later.) The Duc de
Guermantes is as indifferent to Swann's impending death as he is to his
cousin's impending death, and he hurries the Duchesse along. But at the
last moment he sees that the Duchesse is wearing black shoes with a red
dress, and sends her back to change her shoes to match the dress. For this
aristocratic couple only frivolity is serious. The Duc tells Swann, as he
would tell his cousin if he were there, that he is perfectly well.

Like the grandmother's death, Swann's imminent death is touched
with black comedy. Swann is still running little errands for the Duchesse
de Guermantes and laughing at her jokes, even with death so close. And
he does not object in the slightest to the Guermanteses' attitude toward
him, because he understands it so well. He is so used to leading a life of
pleasure that he understands that it is tactless to talk about one's own
death in the midst of all this festivity. He is so tactful that he does not
even say what he is dying of. The only way in which he fails to conform
to the rules of society is by expressing support of Dreyfus. But that he
does only to the narrator, and in a way that the narrator considers so
prejudiced as to be ridiculous. In Proust's view, we cannot be taken
altogether seriously, even on our deathbed. The skull grins.

Chapter Five

Sodome et Gomorrhe (Cities of the Plain)

Part 1

With *Sodome et Gomorrhe* we enter fully into the subject of homosexuality, both male and female, which seemed to Proust so important that he thought of giving this title to several volumes of his work. Throughout, as Melvin Seiden remarks, the narrator maintains the position of a fascinated observer, who does not share the customs of this particular "race," but who likes to think of himself in terms of a botanist studying the reproductive mechanisms of flowers.[1]

His initiation into the hidden world of homosexuality comes completely by accident. While keeping watch for the Duc and Duchesse de Guermantes to return, he also keeps an eye out for the insect that is to pollinate the Duchesse's orchid, which has been set out in the courtyard. He is rewarded by the sight of the unexpected encounter of the Baron de Charlus and Jupien, who are compared to the insect and the orchid, in that their encounter is as providential and as difficult to achieve as the botanical one, since normally they are never in the same place at the same time.

Before the Baron and Jupien see each other, the narrator notices that the Baron, his defenses relaxed, looks very much like a woman. The narrator thinks that he looks more appealing that way, free of his exaggerated cult of virility. The Baron and Jupien catch sight of each other, and proceed to strike attitudes indicative of their mutual attraction. Jupien leaves for work, followed by the Baron, and then the two of them return. They enter Jupien's shop in order to make love. The narrator listens through a partition, much as he had "involuntarily" spied on Mlle Vinteuil and her friend at Montjouvain. He hears the men's orgiastic cries and the sounds of them taking a bath, then listens to their conversation. But, as Compagnon observes, he does not comment on his own voyeurism (302). Overjoyed at finding what he is looking for all the time, the Baron quizzes Jupien to discover if anyone else in the neighborhood is available. Jupien is rather hurt, but does provide the Baron with some information. The Baron informs Jupien of his particular tastes, and mentions the listening narrator himself as one of the young men he is interested in.

As the saying goes, "Listeners hear no good of themselves." What the Baron has to say is hardly flattering to the narrator, particularly when he describes himself as a bishop and the narrator as a braying donkey. Jupien is shocked by the association of homosexuality with religion. Undeterred, the Baron elevates himself to the status of cardinal. The Baron's religious beliefs will be a source of mirth for the narrator throughout the book, for the narrator shares Jupien's attitude.

From this scene between the Baron and Jupien, the narrator, suddenly enlightened on the whole subject of homosexuality, as he had been at Montjouvain on the subject of sadism, begins a disquisition on homosexuals that logically should have required years of research. He describes all manner of homosexuals, recognizable to heterosexuals or the reverse. According to him, the homosexual is a woman who finds herself in the body of a man and therefore naturally seeks out men as sexual partners. This theory, together with the botanical references that continue to abound in this part of the text, is designed to refute the idea that homosexuality is abnormal. The homosexual, for Proust, is natural, but exceptional. The narrator indicates that it is a source of suffering for the homosexual, a suffering with which Proust implicitly invites us to sympathize, that he should find his tastes so hard to gratify, partly because of the lack of suitable male partners and partly because of the disgrace that awaits him if he displays his desires.

Proust gives full rein to his eloquence, adopting tones suitable to a preacher, as he compares the "race" of homosexuals to that of the Jews: both groups struggle under the burden of contempt that the rest of society loads them with, and members of both groups are apparently so assimilated that they despise other members of their "race." The cruelty directed at homosexuals by other members of society is particularly apparent in the case of Oscar Wilde. But all homosexuals, however different they may appear, live with the same opprobrium.

Different types of homosexuals are described. There are those who dress and behave so conservatively that when they join each other in a restaurant, the other diners think they are the members of some respectable society. There are those who wear jewelry and make a spectacle of themselves. There are those who are so convinced of the superiority of homosexuality that they try to convert other men who appear worthy. There are those who are bisexual and even get married. There are those who take mistresses but look so feminine in bed that their mistresses are alarmed. There are those who lead a chaste existence because it seems so impossible to fulfill their desires. There are those who have affairs with lesbians, a notion that appears to have fascinated Proust. But one thing remains constant for all homosexuals: they all recognize each other, and they all live under the crushing burden of an existence whose most necessary joys they must deny at all costs. They are the descendants of those inhabitants of Sodom who successfully convinced the exterminating angel that they were not sodomites—which Proust does not hesitate to consider a good thing.

Finally, the narrator informs us that he did not have all these ideas at the time he was spying on the Baron and Jupien, and that he was sorry to have missed the conjunction of the orchid with the insect by being distracted by that of Charlus with Jupien. So this impassioned tirade, this vehement plea for tolerance and understanding, ends in a kind of pirouette, intended to disarm the reader and prevent him from wondering why the narrator feels so strongly about all this and how he has managed to be so well informed.

Part 2, Chapter 1

After this general introduction to the subject of homosexuality, Proust goes on to introduce us to a variety of individual homosexuals, whom the narrator views with scientific interest and a considerable degree of amusement. The narrator, after his initiation into their world, can spot homosexuals at sight and becomes positively clairaudient when it comes to eavesdropping on their conversations. Just as the death of the narrator's grandmother had its comic side, so these tragic figures become unwitting comedians—as the Baron de Charlus had been for the narrator after the latter's initial bewilderment at Balbec. Partly owing to the narrator's interest in homosexuals, he finds the fête of the Princesse de Guermantes considerably more entertaining than the dinner party of the Duchesse de Guermantes.

This thread is intertwined with that of the narrator's comic uncertainty as to whether he has really been invited to the Princesse's fête, followed by the necessity he is under to find someone to introduce him to the Prince de Guermantes, once it is clear that the Princesse knows who he is and is glad to see him. As Shattuck says, "This is a far cry from the gloomiest book ever written" (83). In his anxiety, he pays particular attention to all the other guests, and seems to be fully informed about everyone. For instance, he knows that the Duc de Châtellerault has had sexual relations with the "barker" whose job it is to announce the guests, but that neither of them knows who his partner was; he knows the whole history of the Marquis de Vaugoubert's platonic homosexuality and why he has such a masculine-looking wife; and he knows how and why Mme d'Arpajon's social position is shaky. Naturally enough, he now knows why the Baron de Charlus has been taking such an interest in him, but so far from disliking him for it, he is sorry that he had neglected the Baron after the latter had been so affectionate toward him. In fact, this positive feeling is not due so much to pure disinterestedness as to the fact that the Baron is about the only person he knows at this garden party who is able to introduce him to the Prince. But the Baron refuses to do so. Finally M. de Bréauté saves him.

This long-sought introduction results only in a brief remark from the Prince, who shortly after closets himself with Swann. Thus the theme of the homosexual mingles with that of the Jew; both are outsiders in the world of the aristocracy, which yet accepts the "closet gay" and the assimilated Jew, so long as the one keeps on his mask and the other does not have the bad taste to declare his support of Dreyfus. No one knows what the Prince de Guermantes is saying to Swann, and there is some speculation that the Prince is telling Swann to leave his house. But the theme of the precarious social position of Swann, the Jew, is intertwined with that of the homosexual, the Marquis de Vaugoubert, who learns with joy from the Baron de Charlus that certain legations are full of homosexuals. However, he does not dare to act on this information, and his frightened concupiscence is made even more comic when the objects of his desire are depicted in terms borrowed from Racine's Old Testament plays.

What the homosexual and the Jew have in common is that they are liable to be excluded at any time. Exclusion is perhaps the principal theme of this garden party—exclusion and humiliation. At the same time it is comic. Mme de d'Arpajon is soaked with water from the Hubert Robert fountain, to the joy of the Grand Duc Wladimir, who follows this up by shouting, "Bravo, la vieille!" (Bravo, old girl!).[2] The party is full of women who, like Mme d'Arpajon, have lost their social position, or who, like Mme de Souvré, are anxious to maintain their social position, or who are at a precarious peak in their social position, like Mme de Surgis-le-Duc, the Duc de Guermanteses' latest mistress, whose sons fascinate the Baron de Charlus. At the secure summit of her social position is the Duchesse de Guermantes, who is constantly bullied and humiliated by her tyrannical and unloving husband, even if he likes to show her off in society.

Swann appears, now looking very much more Jewish, as the result of his illness, than he had done before. At the same time as he looks more Semitic, he also feels more Semitic. After a lifetime of assimilation, he finally feels Jewish and linked to other Jews because of the Dreyfus case. The narrator is amazed to think that this individual once embodied his ideal of prestige. Even so, Swann seems to have changed physically for the worse in a very short time.

Robert de Saint-Loup suddenly turns up and takes hold of the narrator to complain about all the skirt-chasers in his family who have the nerve to teach him how to behave and who have even thought of putting his money in a trust fund. The narrator thinks to himself that the Baron de Charlus really has less to reproach himself with than Robert, quite apart from the fact that he is hardly a skirt-chaser, but he does not express this opinion directly. However, Robert goes on to say that skirt chasing is perfectly all right, an opinion he never would have held when he was in love. He even recommends visiting brothels, particularly one he knows where an aristocratic young lady, Mlle de l'Orgeville, can be found, together with the first chambermaid of Mme de Putbus. These recommendations will linger in the mind of the narrator. Unfortunately, Saint-Loup has to leave very shortly, so he cannot take him to visit the brothel in question.

Meanwhile he comments on the admiration of his uncle for Mme de Surgis-le-Duc, although he does not have the least idea of what has prompted it. This is a Proustian example of how well you can know someone without really knowing him. This axiom has multiple dimensions. For example, the narrator himself does not really know Robert. It all depends on one's perspective—the "lens" through which the reader looks—for the narrator points out that uncles and nephews are very often similar. But Robert has changed in more ways than one. Love affairs now leave him indifferent and he has lost all interest in literature. The earlier Robert had a personality almost entirely based on his love for Rachel; his evolution will present further changes in character.

The Baron de Charlus compliments Mme de Surgis-le-Duc, who is flattered to introduce her sons to him, without realizing that they are the real objects of his attention. Swann joins the narrator and Robert and immediately starts discussing the Dreyfus affair, as he believes that

Robert and the narrator are also Dreyfusards. However, Robert informs him that he is no longer a supporter of Dreyfus. His Dreyfusism, like so much else, has disappeared with his love for Rachel. Now he supports the army. With that revelation he takes off, leaving the narrator with Swann, whom the narrator cannot bring himself to desert. He asks Swann about his conversation with the Prince de Guermantes, but is temporarily distracted by being invited to join Mme de Surgis-le-Duc and the Baron de Charlus, at a little distance. Mme de Saint-Euverte passes by, in search of guests for her garden party, and the Baron seizes the opportunity to heap scatological insults upon her, for the sheer joy of being insolent. This is a fairly typical example of the Baron's conversational style.

Returning to Swann, the narrator listens to his remarks on jealousy without realizing that he himself is fated to be a jealous lover. Then, after a little byplay with Mme de Surgis-le-Duc, Swann tells the story of his conversation with the Prince. Reduced to its essentials, the Prince had told him that he and his wife had come to the conclusion, separately and independently, that Dreyfus is innocent. This account is interrupted, however, by the Duc de Guermantes, who invites the narrator to stay for a select little supper. The narrator refuses, because he has to go home to receive Albertine, to whom he has given a ticket for *Phèdre*. He is not in the least interested in Gilberte, whom Swann suggests he should visit. But since he is on the subject of love, he finds this a suitable moment to let us know that the Princesse de Guermantes is unhappily in love with the Baron de Charlus.

The Duc and Duchesse de Guermantes take the narrator home. Before they leave, the Duc takes the Baron to one side and is extremely affectionate with him, out of gratitude for the Baron's kindness to Mme de Surgis-le-Duc, the Duc's current mistress. The Duchesse de Guermantes, thoroughly annoyed for the same reason, breaks into their conversation, and drags her husband off.

As they return home, the narrator's thoughts are full of Mlle de l'Orgeville and the chambermaid of Mme de Putbus, to the extent that he makes furtive attempts to track them down through the Duc and Duchesse, but to no avail. He does, however, remember that he is expecting the visit of Albertine. He delays just long enough to hear the Duc's relatives announce that the Duc's cousin is dead, to which the Duc, determined not to miss his fancy-dress ball, replies "Mais non, on exagère, on exagère! (People exaggerate!) (*Sodome*, 1:201).

Once home, the narrator learns that Albertine has not arrived. Even though he has just been making humorous remarks about Françoise and her daughter, he quite suddenly settles down to suffer and to wait, just as he had done in Combray. He has a telephone, which has a very quiet ring, and he concentrates all his powers of hearing on it. When it does ring, it reminds him of Wagner's *Tristan and Isolde*, a Proustian hint that a tragic love story is about to begin. Albertine is calling to say that it is too late for her to come. The narrator, devious and tyrannical at once, as he always is to be with her, obliges her to come, although Françoise deeply resents having to get out of bed to let her in, and they spend a while kissing and drinking orangeade. When Albertine leaves, she is now in possession of the wallet decorated with turquoises that Gilberte had once given the narrator and that had been dear to him for that reason. Now that Gilberte means nothing to him, he is perfectly happy to give it away. He feels obliged to write to Gilberte, because Swann had said that Gilberte would like to see him, but he writes this letter in a mood of indifference.

Quite suddenly, without any apparent connection with the subject of Albertine and Gilberte, the narrator informs us that the Duc de Guermantes has been converted to Dreyfusism by three charming ladies at a spa. There is in fact a hidden connection between the former subject and the latter one, the theme of how people can totally change under a new influence. Proust goes on to talk about changes in fashion and their effect on salons, since Mme Swann's salon is becoming very smart. He then discusses changes in politics, artistic performances, and music. Mme Verdurin is attracting notice by her constant presence at the Russian ballet, while Mme Swann is able to count on the assiduity of Bergotte. The narrator wonders if Mme Swann has seen snobbery in his apparent readiness to resume relations with Gilberte, particularly as Gilberte has become an heiress, and consequently a good marriage prospect. But if the narrator continues to visit titled ladies, it is because his imagination has been stirred by their dwellings, one of which reminds him of Combray. Or so he says.

Proust puts the following heading here, but we are still in part 1: *Les Intermittences du Coeur (The Intermittences of the Heart)*. The narrator visits Balbec for the second and last time. The hotel manager thinks highly of him, and favors him with his linguistic lapses on the way back from the station where the manager has come to meet him. Meanwhile, the narrator muses on the chambermaid of the Baronne de Putbus, whom he is pretty sure of meeting at the château the Verdurins have rented from the Cambremers, and on all the pretty girls he is likely to meet at the beach. Saint-Loup has put him in touch with the Cambremers, and the narrator feels that his present social standing is quite impressive.

But his self-congratulatory mood suddenly switches when he is in his
hotel room, which is the same one he had before, for when he bends to
unbutton his half boots, he has a sudden involuntary memory of his
grandmother performing this service for him on their previous stay, and
weeps for her as he had not wept before. The grandmother he had so little
regretted, the one of her last illness, is suddenly replaced by his "real"
grandmother, the one he had always loved. This episode illustrates what
Proust means by an "intermittence of the heart." In all our changes,
which make us so different from ourselves, certain things remain constant but are not always perceptible to us.

He fully realizes for the first time that his grandmother has gone
forever, and he bitterly regrets certain moments when he was unkind to
her. However, even this remorse is dear to him, for it is a proof that he
truly remembers her. His remorse reappears in one of those extremely
lifelike dreams at which Proust excels. In his dream the narrator learns
that the life he would like to attribute to his grandmother is such a
diminished life that it is really death, and consequently he is not allowed
to go and see her, even though he desperately longs to. On waking, he
goes through a kind of *Tristesse d'Olympio* at the thought that the splendid
sea and the splendid beach do not know her. He turns to the wall, but he
is reminded that it is the very wall on which they once tapped messages
to each other. He begs God, if there is a heaven, to let them be together
for eternity. The depth of the narrator's emotion can be measured by the
fact that this is the only time in the whole huge book that he utters a
prayer.

Albertine has left a message indicating that she is near Balbec. She
wants to see him, but he does not want to see anybody. The dowager
Marquise de Cambremer has left her card before proceeding on her
charitable social round of visits to people she does not particularly want
to see. (The implication is that she really does want to see the narrator.)
Mme de Cambremer, at the seaside, is a kind of little Duchesse de
Guermantes for the other inhabitants, even though she has no prestige in
Paris, so she feels obliged to accept all the invitations she receives to make
people happy. However, the narrator does not accept her invitation,
although he would have been glad to do so two days earlier. He has no
more wishes of a worldly kind and is happy to think that he will be able
to commune in his sorrow with his mother, who will be arriving shortly.
But the narrator, looking at himself from a later perspective, has to admit
that his was only a passing grief, while his mother's was a lasting one.

All his passing grief can do, when his mother arrives, is make him recognize how much his mother suffers, and how much her preoccupation with her mother has made her turn into a replica of her. Her chief purpose in coming to Balbec has been to relive the moments her mother spent there. We realize just how passing the narrator's grief is when he starts chatting cheerfully about an old neighbor from Combray and applying certain verses by Racine to the personnel of the hotel. Just as events worthy of Molière accompanied the grandmother's agony, so Racine is frequently quoted by the narrator in a spirit of frivolity, although this will not always be so. At the time of his genuine suffering, later on, he will treat Racine with deadly seriousness.

However, his grief for his grandmother does not disappear all at once. It diminishes gradually, by fits and starts. At one moment he is looking at the photograph Saint-Loup took of his grandmother, feeling no particular emotion and thinking of joining Albertine, when Françoise informs him that on the day his grandmother posed for the photograph she was very ill and had difficulty looking presentable. In fact, she had been ill a lot and had encouraged the narrator to have dinner with Saint-Loup in Rivebelle in order to hide it from him. The hotel manager confirms this account of her illness and reveals that he had been thinking of asking the grandmother to leave the hotel. Naturally, these two pieces of information are painful for the narrator, although his reaction to Françoise is to feel more fondness for her. He has another dream about his grandmother, but she seems even deeper into death this time.

The narrator continues looking at his grandmother's photograph, but his distress diminishes. It is soon time to get together with Albertine again. This particular intermittence of the heart is giving way by fits and starts to another in which the narrator is, he says, wholly absorbed by the beauties of nature, particularly the apple trees in bloom like the pear trees that had accompanied his recognition of Rachel.

Part 2

In this chapter, to use Proust's terminology, Gomorrah joins Sodom. But not immediately, because the narrator continues to trace the line of his fading grief and shows how he begins to hope for happiness with Albertine and even to desire her, although he tries to distract this desire for a while by gazing at the sea. Finally he sets off in search of Albertine. But once he is in the local train he has an involuntary memory of his grandmother and of the distress she had felt when he got slightly drunk in the train from Paris to Balbec on their previous visit. He gets off the train and walks back to Balbec, admiring the hawthorns as he goes. As soon as he gets back to the hotel, he sends Françoise to fetch Albertine. He is a little anxious over the time she takes to come, but when she arrives she appears to be all willingness to answer his beck and call. Françoise, however, announces that Albertine will only cause him grief, a prediction that is all too true.

The Princesse de Parme appears in the dining room of the Grand Hotel. For a moment the narrator takes pleasure in observing her. But he is chiefly preoccupied with girls, and he informs us that he took his pleasure with 13 of Albertine's friends during this stay at Balbec, quite as much as with Albertine, although he wanted Albertine from time to time. He has no suspicions to arouse his anxious doubts where she is concerned until Dr. Cottard, one day at the Casino of Incarville, watching Andrée and Albertine dancing together, remarks that their breasts are touching and they must be reaching orgasm.

It takes a while for the suffering this remark causes the narrator to sink in. At the same time he is gradually becoming attached to Albertine because of the excuses she makes to avoid seeing him whenever he wants. (It is a Proustian axiom noticed before that people always want to see those people who show that they are not particularly keen on seeing them.) When Albertine sees the narrator, she appears excited by his presence, but this does not jibe with her eagerness to go and see someone else. The narrator's questions about the other person she has to go and see are already beginning to take on the inquisitorial tone of the questions he is to ask later on, when it will be a matter of life and death to him to find out what she is concealing from him—particularly her lesbianism. In fact, it is not long before the name of Sappho enters the discussion, even on this relatively peaceful occasion.

A few days later the narrator will be in the Casino of Balbec with Andrée and Albertine when Bloch's sister and a girl cousin come in and make an exhibition of their lesbianism. The cousin is well known at Balbec for having an affair with an actress. Andrée expresses virtuous indignation, and she and Albertine turn their backs on the guilty pair, but Albertine lets slip that she had been watching them in a mirror all the time they were there.

Albertine's actions would seem to confirm Cottard's opinion of her lesbianism, but oddly enough the narrator claims not to share it. When he joins Andrée at Elstir's house, he is so impressed by her poise and dignity that he cannot believe she is a lesbian—at any rate for the moment. These suspicions come and go, as he remembers what he has been told of Mme Swann, and he mentally notes that he is glad that he is not in love with Albertine. He demonstrates to himself and Albertine that he is not in love with her by addressing offensive remarks to her the next time he sees her while being extremely pleasant to Andrée.

At this point the Cambremers turn up, and the narrator's mother seeks refuge inside the hotel. There is a very comic description of the way in which the dowager Marquise de Cambremer has adorned herself to be worthy of her social duties. Her daughter-in-law is all smiles because she has heard from Robert de Saint-Loup that the narrator is on close terms with the Guermantes family. The narrator remarks that this is the descent of the Cambremers that his grandmother had been afraid of, but notes that it had happened quite differently from the way she had expected. This episode in itself is hardly worth mentioning, except that it is an illustration of the Proustian axiom that certain events that do not at first seem possible to the objective observer do in fact come to pass, but in quite different ways than one would have expected. In fact this axiom has been true of the narrator's whole dealings with the Guermantes family, not to mention Gilberte and Bergotte, but it suits Proust's sense of humor to underline it, at this point, with reference to the Cambremers.

The conversation between the narrator, the dowager Marquise de Cambremer, the young Marquise de Cambremer, and their guest, a lawyer, is highly entertaining. The dowager Marquise has a true appreciation of the arts but which makes her drool, the young Marquise is a fervent defender of the avant-garde but has no real appreciation of anything that is not fashionable, the lawyer has the bad taste to admire Le Sidaner, and the narrator has the advantage of calmly understanding what he admires while coolly toppling the young Marquise's prejudices. Albertine is present but has very little to say. Presumably she is admiring the narrator's self-assurance—that is, if her mind is not on something else. At any rate, she has nothing to say when the young Marquise and the lawyer criticize Elstir, whom she knows and admires. But then, as a *jeune fille*, she is not supposed to push herself forward. She only opens up a little when she has an opportunity to talk about the seagulls, which remind her of Amsterdam; she leaves it to her boyfriend to be an arbiter in matters of taste. In fact, he gives the reader the benefit of his considered views on changes in artistic fashions rather than lecturing his immediate audience. However, out of the kindness of his heart, he does tell the young Marquise that Debussy admires Chopin, for she had always despised her mother-in-law for her devotion to Chopin.

This select company having departed, the narrator takes Albertine up to his room. This man who hates being lied to is a very skillful liar himself, as Howard Moss observes.[3] When Albertine asks him what he has against her, he proceeds to spin a long tale about how he is in love with Andrée and has come to resent Albertine because he has been told that she had sexual relations with Andrée. He obtains a spirited denial from Albertine, and then feels free to be affectionate with her. At the same time, he has obtained from Albertine a refusal to leave him in order to go and have dinner with her aunt. Thus he has succeeded in dominating her more completely than ever before—a need for dominance being one of the salient characteristics of what Proust calls love. In the narrator's opinion he should have left Albertine then and lived with the memory of what had at least seemed to be the love that he had succeeded in inspiring, for he is not a being for whom reciprocal love is possible.

Given the narrator's temperament, it is not surprising that his actual reaction to this high point in their relationship, if it is not to avoid Albertine completely, is to spend more time with his mother, who reminisces to him about his grandmother and their days in Combray. In order to revive his memory of their painted plates illustrating the *Arabian Nights*, his mother, at his request, orders for him the two French translations of the *Arabian Nights*, by Galland and Mardrus, but is shocked by the obscenity of the latter. This little episode has more importance than one might think, for in *Le Temps retrouvé* the narrator speaks of writing a new *Arabian Nights*.

However, the narrator does manage to have solitary strolls with Albertine, in between getting the Dutch courage to issue invitations to other girls he fancies. But as more girls arrive at Balbec, the more afraid he becomes that Albertine is going to take an interest in one of them. He is particularly worried that Mme de Putbus's chambermaid, whom he had not so long ago wanted for himself, will join forces with Albertine, to the point where he would like to get that chambermaid dismissed. Meanwhile Albertine and Andrée are very careful to dispel the narrator's doubts about them.

Around this time, Bloch's sister makes love with a former actress in the dance hall, causing a scandal that, however, has no unpleasant consequences for them, because M. Nissim Bernard, Bloch's uncle, who is homosexual himself, is able to pull strings for them. It is interesting to see how the novel's tone changes from one of anxiety and alarm to that of tolerant amusement as soon as we pass from female to male homosexuality. But we pass again from this topic to a conversation between the narrator and Marie Gineste and Céleste Albaret, two sisters whom Proust knew in real life, for no apparent reason but for the fun of it. Then we come back to the shameless lesbian pair whom Bloch ignores in the street while the narrator expresses his fears that their indecent utterances are addressed to Albertine.

(The Flammarion edition here begins a new volume, but this is simply for convenience of publication. We are in fact going on with Proust's second part, and the subject is not changed.)

The narrator has seen on the beach a young woman with eyes luminous with desire, and has fancied her for himself. He is extremely disconcerted to discover that her starry gaze is fixed on Albertine, who studiously ignores her. The narrator goes on to state that Balbec is full of lesbians whose eyes meet, forming phosphorescent tracks. This is one of the moments when one wonders whether Proust intended us to think that the narrator has become seriously unbalanced, owing to his preoccupation with lesbians, and is not to be taken literally, even though at other times he seems to be so knowing and wise. He goes on to say that the starry-eyed young woman, seeing that Albertine is no longer accessible, takes up with Bloch's cousin instead. But Albertine's reserved manner with other girls seems to the narrator like a ruse intended to throw him off the track. In fact, she arouses his suspicions much more than she calms them. Then, suddenly, his suspicions cease—at least those concerned with lesbianism.

The narrator goes on to tell us how this came to pass, although he pauses first to relate how M. Nissim Bernard had had so much trouble from mixing up two tomato-headed twins, one of whom was heterosexual and the other homosexual, that he had taken a strong dislike to tomatoes. After this fooling, one day the narrator and Albertine get on the local train and are met at the Doncières station by Robert de Saint-Loup, to whom Albertine makes numerous overtures while neglecting the narrator. Before getting on the train, the narrator had already received an invitation from Mme Verdurin, which he had requested in order to find out if the Baronne de Putbus and her chambermaid were staying with her, but now his chief thought is to keep Albertine away from Robert de Saint-Loup.

After Robert de Saint-Loup has left the station, the narrator espies the Baron de Charlus, who was intending to take the train to Paris, but now drops everything when faced with Morel in military uniform and with the insignia of a regimental band. (Morel is doing the two year military service required of all young French men in good health. Like Saint-Loup, he is stationed at Doncières.) The Baron is not quite certain if he will find Morel responsive, so he sends the narrator to fetch him, then joins him himself when the narrator wastes time in the pleasure of meeting an old acquaintance. So a great love affair begins. The narrator gives some thought to this relationship as the local train gets under way, but naturally far more to Albertine and Saint-Loup.

Two days later the narrator is in the local train once more, this time without Albertine, on his way to La Raspelière, the country house Mme Verdurin has rented from the Cambremers. Brichot, Cottard, Saniette, and the sculptor Ski join him. The narrator has presumably heard about Brichot and Saniette from Swann, for he recognizes them (and, of course, Cottard is well known to him), but as the journey continues we are treated to a flood of information about them and the Princesse Sherbatoff, who has not yet got on, which goes beyond anything the narrator can possibly have known at that moment, particularly as the Princesse Sherbatoff, a recent recruit of the Verdurins and the most faithful of the faithful, is someone he had seen in the train while traveling with Albertine and had mistaken for the madam of a brothel. Thus we learn that Cottard once refused to bind up a severe cut on his servant's arm because he was dressed to go out; that Mme Verdurin had got rid of the laundress with whom Brichot was having an affair and that Brichot's sight is going; that Saniette is more timid than ever; and that Ski, who has replaced Elstir as the Verdurins' painter protégé, is a jack of all trades and master of none, while the Princesse Sherbatoff clings to Mme Verdurin because hardly anyone else will associate with her.

The habitués of the Verdurin circle discuss how the violinist who had recently started playing for the circle failed to arrive two nights earlier. Brichot explains a great many etymologies to the narrator, correcting the explanations of the *curé* of Combray, who had spent some time in the region of Balbec and then gone back to Combray. The narrator is fascinated. Then Cottard, Brichot, Saniette, Ski, and the narrator go in search of the Princesse Sherbatoff who informs them that the violinist will be coming that evening with an old friend of his father's. At the same time, the news spreads that Dechambre, the Verdurins' old pianist, is dead. By the time the group arrives at La Raspelière, they have been warned not mention Dechambre to Mme Verdurin, for fear of upsetting her. In truth, she is completely indifferent to the death of her friends and does not want to go to the bother of pretending to mourn them.

She is quite satisfied with the living and is looking forward to the arrival of Morel, in the company of the Baron de Charlus. Ski is surprised to hear that the Baron de Charlus is coming, since in Ski's circle the

Baron has a very bad reputation, but Mme Verdurin, determined to have Morel as a guest, refuses to listen to him. M. de Charlus enters, preceding the Cambremers and looking very ladylike, with Morel, whose virtuosity as a violinist the Baron is to develop in the most surprising manner. Charlus is potentially an impresario in the style of Diaghilev.

The dinner-party scene that follows might have been described by Pascal, for it is marked by acute pessimism about human nature. In "Un Amour de Swann" we had heard quite a lot about the Verdurins and their circle, and what we heard was not to their credit. But now the will to power and dominance that characterizes the Verdurin circle, uninhibited by the veneer of politeness that masks the same traits in aristocratic circles, flourishes unrestrained. The setting is beautiful; the furniture, ornaments, and china are chosen with taste; the cooking is sumptuous; and "only man is vile."[4]

Saniette, who is all meekness, is deliberately tortured by the Verdurins. Surprisingly, Brichot has become another subject for malevolence, and only the narrator is interested in his etymologies. Charlus thinks Cottard has a sexual interest in him, and snubs him because he does not find him attractive, while Cottard, on learning that Charlus is homosexual, thinks he will have to protect his virtue. Morel gets the narrator to enhance the social position of Morel's father, and then snubs him. The Verdurins place the Cambremers above Charlus at table, and Charlus tells M. Verdurin he does not mind because the Verdurins are obviously ignorant of social usage. Later, he goes out of his way to insist on his noble lineage, but for the benefit of Morel rather than of the Verdurins. He even boasts about his patron saint, the Archangel Michael. Mme Verdurin tries being sarcastic with him about his claims to nobility, but he knows how to defend himself.

Cottard snubs M. de Cambremer for being ignorant of medicine; a moment before M. de Cambremer had been about to snub Cottard for being common. But the Baron accompanies Morel on the piano, with great skill and taste. The musical taste of the Verdurin circle is revealed as ignorant and shallow when Morel, asked for Debussy, plays Meyerbeer instead and no one notices the difference. The party winds up when Cottard torments his wife for falling asleep after dinner. The only guests who does not appear to be despised or to despise the others are a Norwegian philosopher, who is but a transitory guest, and the narrator, who spends part of his time thinking about his mother's statement that Albertine's relatives would like him to marry her, and another part admiring mediocre things about La Raspelière in a way that infuriates the younger Mme de Cambremer. But Mme Verdurin has taken a fancy to him and wants him to be part of the circle and bring his "cousin" (Albertine). She warns him at all costs to stay away from the Cambremers, who might keep him from coming to her. However, the narrator has no particular wish to spend time with the Cambremers, for the younger Mme de Cambremer likes to discomfit people, while her husband looks on laughing.

Part 3

Just by way of letting us know that human nature is the same in every social circle, the bellboy who takes the narrator to his room boasts of his sister, who is the mistress of a rich man and relieves herself in very unsuitable places to give others the job of cleaning up. Without giving this piece of information another thought, the narrator treats us to his views on sleep, memory, and life before life and after death. From this he passes to M. de Charlus, who enters the dining room of the Grand Hotel at Balbec in the company of a servant who, although he is dressed like a dandy, is recognized as a servant by the waiters. Aimé, the maître d'hôtel, in particular, asks who the Baron de Charlus is. When the narrator names him, Aimé shows the narrator a very strange letter that the Baron had sent him and that he did not understand, reproaching him for not responding to his advances. Now that Aimé understands what the letter is about, he feels he has missed a golden opportunity. But in the meantime Morel has come along.

For the next 50 pages, the narrator gives us little vignettes of M. de Charlus, Morel, Mme Verdurin, and Saniette, interspersed with lengthy accounts of his excursions with Albertine in a hired car, nights spent kissing her on the dunes, and hours when he settles her down to paint and goes off himself. The narrator points to underground currents when he tells us that the chauffeur and Morel are hand in glove, although they pretend not to know each other, and that they have arranged to get the Verdurins' coachman dismissed so that the chauffeur can take his place. Albertine is also on intimate terms with the chauffeur, but the narrator is unaware of all this at the time, and will hire him on his return to Paris. In the background, the narrator's mother is very distressed about her son's continued intimacy with Albertine, but dares not nag him about it. Saint-Loup is somewhere in the background too, upset that the narrator will only allow him occasional visits. In the midst of the excursions with Albertine there appears a passage in which the narrator, on horseback, watches a plane above him and is moved to tears. This emotion is not explained, but it seems to be a premonition of an autobiographical nature.

Then, after this relative calm, things liven up in the little train on its way to La Raspelière, as Cottard spreads the word that according to Ski M. de Charlus is homosexual. Mme Cottard, misunderstanding what her husband is muttering, goes out of her way to be nice to this Jew, which is what she takes the Baron to be. In fact, the Christian faith of the Baron de Charlus is quite medieval in its literalness. But the other travelers, indifferent to his religious beliefs, become more and more fascinated by his homosexuality and try to get him to talk about it. Mme Verdurin herself varies between making things easy for the Baron and Morel and making rude remarks about them. When the Baron opens up, he discusses Balzac and his treatment of homosexuality. Brichot, with his lively curiosity, seems particularly interested. But Charlus refuses to discuss these topics in front of Morel, for his feelings for the young man are platonic. Besides, he is afraid that Morel's relatives will intervene if he is saddled with a bad reputation.

Just as Saint-Loup loved Rachel more than she loved him, and her acting career was all-important to her, so the Baron de Charlus loves Morel more than Morel loves him, and Morel's status at the Conservatoire is all-important to him. Consequently the way the two couples behave is very similar. But the crazy character of the Baron involves him in episodes that look much funnier to the narrator than Saint-Loup's love affair, as in the example of the duel the Baron invents to get Morel to spend an evening with him.

M. de Charlus is so comic that it must have caused Proust extreme pain to invite us to laugh at him. Next Proust has fun at Dr. Cottard's expense; one of the seconds at the imaginary duel, Dr. Cottard, is afraid he is going to be raped. In fact, he need not worry in the least. But ridicule promptly falls on the Baron again as he compares himself to the Archangel Raphael and Morel to the young Tobias, and yells "Alleluia" in the street.

He is definitely not shouting Alleluia when he learns that someone, actually the Prince de Guermantes acting incognito, has hired Morel to spend the night with him in the brothel of Maineville. He summons Jupien, who arranges for the Baron and himself to watch Morel with his lover (whose identity the Baron does not know) in the brothel. However, everything is ruined because Morel has been warned, and the Baron only sees him, looking like a ghost with terror, in the company of three women. The Prince de Guermantes invites Morel to join him in the little

house he has rented. When Morel arrives, he is overcome by panic at the
sight of the same family photographs he is used to seeing around the
Baron de Charlus, and particularly at the sight of one of the Baron de
Charlus himself. He thinks he has been lured into a trap, and runs away
as fast as he can.

Proust drops this subject for the time being, and the narrator tells us
how he entertains a ruined nobleman, the Comte de Crécy. He does not
mention Odette de Crécy to him, but in fact the Comte de Crécy was
Odette's first husband and it was probably by her that he was ruined,
although the narrator does not know at this point that they were
connected.

From there he goes on to a dinner party to which the Cambremers had
invited Dr. Cottard and Morel. Mme Verdurin obliged the former to
decline, and Morel, who believed the Baron's statement that this minor
nobility was beneath contempt, also declined at the last moment. But
not everyone in the Verdurin circle despises the Cambremers, for Brichot
is in love with the young Marquise. Mme Verdurin breaks up this
burgeoning love affair, but Brichot is so unhappy about it that he
becomes ill and almost loses what is left of his sight. Then the Cambremers invite M. de Charlus, twice, the second time through Morel, but
only Morel turns up, on behalf of the Baron. Then M. de Cambremer goes
to dinner with the Verdurins but leaves his wife behind. The whole thing
turns into a quarrel, which the Cambremers justify by saying that the
Guermantes family is pro-Dreyfus and Mme Verdurin is a social climber.

Then we are back in the little train, going to and from La Raspelière.
The train stops at Doncières and Saint-Loup gets in. Bloch also puts in an
appearance, and asks the narrator to get out to greet Bloch's father. But
the narrator dares not leave Saint-Loup and Albertine alone, even for a
few minutes, and apparently loses Bloch's friendship as a consequence,
for Bloch thinks he is a snob. Not that Bloch's friendship is that valuable,
because Bloch does nothing to support him in front of other people, such
as Albertine's aunt. In any case, their friendship will eventually resume as
if nothing had happened. M. de Charlus is very taken by Bloch and
cunningly questions the narrator about Bloch's address, while making
anti-Semitic remarks to conceal his interest. Morel, on the other hand, is
delighted to see Bloch go.

Proust concludes this chapter by having his narrator say that the
region around Balbec and the châteaux of this region had become so
familiar to him that all the poetry had gone out of them, that he was

thinking in a purely practical way, and that the idea of marrying Albertine seemed absurd.

Part 4

The narrator informs us that he has made his mother happy by deciding not to marry Albertine. He has decided to court Andrée, according to his usual bizarre method of telling her he is not in love with her, and drop Albertine, but puts off telling Albertine he wants to break with her. Instead he starts telling her that he wants to get music by Vinteuil played for him at La Raspelière, and adds that the name Vinteuil probably means nothing to her. She protests that she is on the closest possible terms with Mlle Vinteuil and her best friend and has been for years. The narrator is in a state of shock, as the vision of the scene he once witnessed at Montjouvain rises before him, and he feels that he is being punished for some terrible offence. Joined to the memory of Montjouvain is his memory of what he has been told of Swann's love life. Albertine suddenly becomes acutely necessary to him, and he gets her to spend the night at the hotel, where he grieves. He expects to suffer unceasingly for the rest of his life, now that he is quite sure of the relationship between Albertine and Andrée.

He is joined in his room by Albertine. He tells her one of his typical lies, about a women he claims to be unhappily in love with, to gain her sympathy and be able to weep in front of her without admitting the real reason. In her good-hearted way she offers to spend the night with him. She is his suffering and his only remedy, at the same time. He is determined to take her to Paris, not that Paris is free of lesbians, but because his jealousy is specifically concentrated on Mlle Vinteuil and her friend, and he has to get Albertine away from them at all costs. His jealousy of Saint-Loup was nothing compared to this, because another man would be a rival he could hope to defeat, whereas he cannot hope to appeal to Albertine in the same way as another woman. He cannot even imagine exactly what the appeal of another woman would be.

Because she wants to join Mlle Vinteuil's friend in Trieste for Christmas, he would like to lock her up and take all her money away. In fact, he *will* lock her up, in the next volume, but such imprisonment will do him no good. His other wish, to burn Trieste down, is less feasible. Staying in Balbec is impossible, because there she can see Bloch's cousins. So he suggests that she come with him to Paris. His mother will be away, visiting a dying great-aunt in Combray. And he tempts Albertine with the idea that his wife would have a car and a yacht, without revealing that he is in love with her. However, he does say that she can calm his sorrow by being constantly with him. The examples of Swann and Saint-Loup have made him believe that no one can love him except for his money.

Albertine leaves for a moment and then lets the narrator know, through the elevator boy, that she can go with him to Paris that very day. The news of his planned departure gets around, and that day the hotel manager, Marie Gineste, Cécile Albaret, M. de Cambremer, M. de Crécy, and Mme Verdurin all urge him to stay, to his annoyance. However, he does have a moment when he thinks that his emotions are insane. He thinks that he would only need a little willpower to live in a purely intellectual world, which would be the real one, for his loves have never been based on the real merits of the women concerned.

A bloody sun rises, the symbol of the daily sacrifice he will have to make. As he weeps, his mother enters, looking distressed and very like his grandmother. But nothing seems real to him except that long-ago scene at Montjouvain, and he tells his mother that he cannot go on living without marrying Albertine.

Chapter Six
La Prisonnière (The Captive)

This volume begins on a comparatively cheerful note, with the narrator waking in Paris to the sunshine, sure that he has Albertine under control, and that every night she will give him a kiss to calm him, as his mother's goodnight kiss had calmed him in Combray. However, this is far from being a calm or cheerful volume. Endlessly Proust rings the changes on the narrator's variations as he alternates between jealousy and satiety, his wish to get rid of Albertine and his wish to hang on to her at all costs. As the narrator is to say of the music of Vinteuil and of Wagner, it seems less like the return of a motif than of a fit of neuralgia. But there is no clumsiness involved, nor did the narrator intend to denigrate Vinteuil or Wagner when he used this comparison. On the contrary, Proust wishes to show us, as on a barometer, the level of the narrator's feelings, hour by hour and day by day. He wishes us to partake of the narrator's torment, and so we do, until we find blessed relief in those moments when he allows us to think of something else.

Although we know so much about other characters in the book, whose secrets the narrator penetrates with a glance, Albertine remains a mystery because the narrator is incapable of viewing her with the objective interest that he brings to the other characters. As Moss says, the narrator's greatest lie is that he is objective in regard to the truth where Albertine is concerned (52). He tries to solve her riddle by means that seem mathematical rather than intuitive, and fails. I feel like saying to him, as the Italian prostitute said to Rousseau, "Lascia le donne, e studia la matematica" (Leave women alone and study mathematics).[1] And, indeed, this vast error on the part of the narrator seems to be intended by Proust. It is a case of "How are the mighty fallen!" Because the narrator has indulged his nerves and failed to use his willpower one time too many, he must suffer as Swann had suffered, and his knowledge of what Swann went through and why is of no practical use to him.

But immediately here the narrative concerns the narrator's search in vain, in Le Figaro, for an article he had submitted that was a reworking of his steeples of Martinville sketch, and a letter from his mother, who is very distressed that Albertine should be living with the narrator in the family apartment. But the very values of Combray prevent the narrator's mother from interfering, just as Françoise refuses to allow Albertine to make any noise before the narrator is awake.

Oddly enough, the narrator's suspicions about Albertine and Andrée seem to have disappeared, because he sends Albertine out on car rides with Andrée and the Verdurins' chauffeur, who as we noticed earlier is a friend of Morel. Albertine seems to be enjoying herself at this point. She has become more intelligent (not that the narrator cares much about that) and quotes from Racine's *Esther* when she finally dares to go in and see the narrator. She talks about going to the Buttes-Chaumont, but the narrator relies on Andrée to tell him where they have really been, particularly as Albertine tells him that Andrée was once in love with him. But, just in case, he suggests going to Saint-Cloud instead. He then questions her, out of the blue, about her relations with Gilberte Swann, and next expresses such a strong desire to see the Sainte Chapelle again that she suggests going with him, after which he feels free to stay in bed. The narrator is very contradictory. It is no wonder Albertine eventually tires of him—and at the back of the narrator we seem to see Proust himself, grieving over the way the narrator spoils things for himself by yielding to his neurotic impulses. However, he does seem to approve of the narrator's taste for solitude, which could allow him to be creative, even if he wastes his solitude with desire for other women and wishes that Albertine would go back to her aunt.

His jealousy is intermittent. He notes that if he could have supervised Albertine's pleasures or if she had indulged in them in another country, he would not have minded. Probably he imagines this. However, in his calmer moments, when Albertine does not seem like a nuisance, he tries to please her. Since Albertine is very fashion-conscious, he frequently calls on the Duchesse de Guermantes to get ideas for clothes for Albertine. On one of these occasions an at-home gown by the designer Fortuny is mentioned for the first time, while the Duc makes anti-Semitic remarks that do not seem to tally at all with his conversion to the cause of Dreyfus. The narrator finds it safer to stick to clothes, and asks the Duchesse about her golden slippers.

The narrator, on his way home, runs into M. de Charlus and Morel on their way to visit Jupien, to whose niece Morel has become engaged. The Baron feels that he is going to have a family of his own. But Morel's neurotic character might prevent the marriage from taking place.

On one of his visits to the Duchesse, the narrator receives some syringas as a gift from her. As he carries them back to the apartment, he runs into Andrée, who tells him that Albertine cannot stand strong odors. This small episode seems completely inconsequential, but the day will come when the narrator reinterprets the behavior of the two young women in a very distressing way. In fact, Albertine and Andrée had just been making love, and the fuss about the syringas serves as a screening device to conceal their emotions. Another concealment takes place shortly, when Andrée replies to the narrator's questions about how she and Albertine have spent their time on their latest outing, and gives him answers that only arouse fresh suspicions. Another detail that seems as inconsequential as the syringa episode concerns Albertine's new gold ring, which she says her aunt gave her. Although the narrator does not suspect it at the moment, the ring probably came from a lover.

But the narrator is fully aware that Albertine, who has become so docile, is no longer the free spirit he had loved by the sea. Neither are the other members of the *petite bande* what they once were. Connected with this realization is the pleasure the narrator derives from watching Albertine asleep, when the riddle of her personality no longer perplexes him. He even masturbates against her in her sleep, when there is no possibility of her evading his will so long as he does not awaken her. It is only at such moments that he can fully enjoy Albertine while remaining completely calm, or, in other words, that he can exercise complete dominance without meeting even a mental resistance.

This is all very peculiar. The narrator is disconcerted to realize that he is becoming increasingly similar to the most peculiar member of his family, Aunt Léonie, in that it has become almost impossible for him to get out of bed. One might add that Aunt Léonie's jealous doubts of the integrity of Françoise and then Eulalie are also being repeated with a different cast. This duplication fits in with Proust's belief in the power of heredity. As one grows older, one becomes like all one's relatives, but usually like one in particular. As the narrator lies in bed he broods about Albertine and her concealments.

Her intention to visit Mme Verdurin gives him a lot to think about. He is sure this visit involves a reason he would disapprove of, because she was so annoyed when he tried to dissuade her from going. He calls Andrée on the phone to ask her to take Albertine anywhere the following day except to see Mme Verdurin. André replies that Albertine has to see Mme Verdurin, so then the narrator suggests going with them. Andrée does not care for this idea at all, so the narrator hangs up. Albertine is not at all happy either about this telephone call, and tries to discourage the narrator from accompanying her and Andrée, while suggesting that she may not go to see Mme Verdurin after all.

The narrator occasionally gets out of bed to go for a walk with Albertine. These walks invariably end at an airport, much to the satisfaction of both of them. The narrator says that a plane represents liberty for him. Possibly it does for Albertine too. At any rate, the narrator suspects that she is lying when she says that she will not visit the Verdurins. He tries to cut off her retreat by getting her to go to a show at the Trocadéro instead. He is well aware that he is making both of them unhappy, and sums up the situation by telling the reader, "J'appelle ici amour une torture réciproque" (What I here call love is reciprocal torture).[2] But Albertine plays her part by contradicting her former lies to him, which she has forgotten, so that everything she says seems like a lie and foments the jealousy on which his love depends.

His jealous questions—such as whether Albertine knows Bloch's cousin Esther—now explode as unexpectedly as a time bomb. But he is egotistical enough to be aware only of his own anguish. He respects Françoise for having told him at Balbec, "Je vois bien le caractère qu'elle a, elle vous fera des chagrins" (I can very well see the kind of character she has, she will make you suffer) (*Sodome*, 1:274). The whole *drame du coucher* of Combray comes to life again, centered round Albertine. He is even jealous of the people of whom she seems to be dreaming, such as Andrée.

From time to time Proust allows us a brief respite from this interminable brooding. Such an episode occurs at this point when the narrator awakens to hear the cries of the vendors in the street below. Albertine joins him, and enjoys the street cries with him. Naturally, it is at this moment that he utters the ominous words that she might have a riding accident. Not that he wishes it, but he does wish that she would go away and never come back. But then her wish to buy ice cream at Rebattet's reactivates his jealousy, because Rebattet's is where the Verdurins buy their ice cream. She proceeds to describe the pleasure she takes in eating ice cream in a way that seems to him unnervingly voluptuous and excessively literary; indeed, her description bears the imprint of his own style. He has had an effect on her, he realizes with surprise, although not the effect he would have wished.

The time for Albertine to go to the Trocadéro approaches. The narrator is glad that Andrée is going with her, because he has lost confidence in the chauffeur. He does not entirely trust the chauffeur's account of their trip to Versailles, although it does not as yet occur to him to have any doubts about Albertine's three-day trip to Balbec with the chauffeur, a trip documented by a rain of postcards.

Meanwhile, the narrator indulges an interest in little working-class girls. He considers this interest perfectly innocent, but, when he carries it further later on, it will get him in trouble with the police. As the French say, he has two weights and two measures. Just as he has finished reading a letter from his mother, who concludes by reproaching him, in terms borrowed from Mme de Sévigné, for his extravagance, Françoise ushers in a little milk girl, whom the narrator pretends to have summoned to carry a letter for him. He is so disturbed by her presence that, to conceal his emotion, he picks up the newspaper, and reads that Léa will be performing at the Trocadéro that afternoon.

He has every reason to suspect that Léa is lesbian and that Albertine knows her, or any rate knows her girlfriends. This blow makes him send away the milk girl after giving her a handsome tip, for now he can think only of how to prevent Albertine from meeting Léa's friends at the Trocadéro. One nail drives out another, and he is no longer concerned with Mme Verdurin or Mlle Vinteuil. He sends Françoise to bring Albertine back from the Trocadéro, with a lying letter saying that he has been upset by a letter from the woman with whom he is in love and about whom he told her during their last night in Balbec. Françoise succeeds in her mission, and the narrator is glad to see that he has Albertine so much under control. Consequently she ceases to interest him, for the time being.

Taking advantage of his new peace of mind, the narrator starts playing Vinteuil's sonata on the piano. He wonders whether he has given up something real by giving up a literary career, and is inclined to think that he has. Vinteuil reminds him of Wagner, whose *Tristan and Isolde* he begins to play, and he has no doubt for the moment that Wagner's music is real, because of the visceral nature of his leitmotifs. Unlike Albertine, this music helps him to go down into himself and discover something new. The great artists, whether musicians or painters, convey a qualitative difference that we could never discover through love. He goes on from this thought to discuss the self-reflective nature of the great creators of the nineteenth century when they considered their works and turned them into cycles. This is particularly true of Wagner, and the narrator thinks of the moment when Wagner incorporates the shepherd's air in *Tristan and Isolde.* But does this kind of artistic success come more from hard work than from a perception of a higher reality? If so, the narrator need not regret having sacrificed art for life. He goes on playing Wagner, and participates in Wagner's creative joy.

Suddenly the narrator begins to think of Morel and the anxiety he causes M. de Charlus by his claim that he is not free in the evenings because he is taking a course in algebra. This is an obvious lie, and the Baron tries vainly to decipher the reality concealed beneath this lie. But the Baron's social life, which is extremely active, does not allow him time to brood as much as the narrator does. Neither does the Baron reflect on the attacks of nervous spite to which Morel is subject. But the narrator witnesses one when he passes in front of Jupien's shop, having left the piano, and hears Morel screaming "Grand pied de grue" at his fiancée (this is not even French, but it means "filthy trollop") (*La Prisonnière*, 292).

Albertine arrives, and the narrator goes for a ride with her. This time he notices a ruby ring on her finger. She claims to have bought it. He discusses Elstir with her, and claims that Elstir is in contradiction with his own impressionism in preferring to look at genuinely antique buildings instead of seeing beauty everywhere. They arrive at the Bois de Boulogne and stroll together, but the narrator is determined to go home again as quickly as possible because he has decided to visit Mme Verdurin that evening, in order to find out whom Albertine could have wanted to see at the Verdurins that afternoon. In the meantime both Albertine and the narrator gaze at the beautiful young women around them, and the narrator wishes he were free to follow them. Doubtless Albertine does too. This makes her more attractive to him, for the moment, as his jealousy once more enters into play.

At home she is his prisoner, and resents it. In a sense, he is her prisoner too, for if it were not for the necessity of controlling her movements he could be in Venice, a trip he has been wanting to take, without doing anything about it, for years. Albertine is showing signs of wanting her freedom back. She is up to something with Gisèle. The narrator does not know what, but her wish for liberty may have something to do with it. He would like to break off their relationship, but procrastinates and thinks of gifts he can bestow on Albertine, such as a Fortuny gown or even a yacht.

At this point the theme of great artistic creation breaks in again, in contrast to the unsatisfactory nature of love, as we learn of the death of Bergotte. This death has a more than usually macabre interest, in that Proust is said to have used his own experience on his deathbed to add some telling details—probably the unusually vivid nightmares Bergotte had in his last nights. Proust's resentment against his doctors had also influenced this episode. Bergotte also shares the narrator's penchant for little girls, to whom he pays large sums of money for a few caresses. But his death is as artistic as his writing has been, for he dies at a Vermeer exhibition, rapt in contemplation of Vermeer's *View of Delft*, and particularly of a little patch of yellow wall that is so well painted that it puts his latest books to shame. He feels, at the moment of his death, that he has rashly exchanged his life for the little patch of yellow wall. But he may have returned to the better world from which we possibly come, bringing its values. His books keep angelic vigil in shop windows and seem to be the symbol of his resurrection, even though Proust also notes in this passage that there will be a time when no human beings are left to read.

There is a discrepancy between the date of Bergotte's death, when the narrator came to learn of it, and the date given in the newspapers, because Albertine claims to have met Bergotte and talked to him the day he was reported to have died. For a long time the narrator believes Albertine, because she lies so simply and naturally. But eventually he finds her out by using his detective instincts. It would be interesting to know exactly what Albertine thinks of the narrator's lies, because, after all his self-righteous comments about her lies, he sets out for the Verdurins' after telling her that he is going to visit some of his aristocratic friends and inviting her to come with him. But she says she has nothing to wear and her hairstyle is unbecoming, so the narrator sets off alone, glorying in having made Albertine unattractive.

A long passage follows, one full of the animation that the reader really needs after all this brooding. The events that come to pass are not in the least happy or edifying, but they take place outside the narrator's mind. Thus, within the context of the fiction they appear real, and they are exciting. All this gives us a breathing space before we get back to the narrator's miserable relationship with Albertine again.

The first person the narrator meets is Morel, sitting by the side of the road and weeping convulsively for shame at having treated his fiancée badly. But the narrator has no assurance that this regret will last. In other words, Morel is not quite sane. His screams of rage had been provoked by her unwillingness to become first his mistress and then his procuress. Since the Baron de Charlus is too moral to approve of this behavior, Morel is thinking of dropping the Baron, Jupien, and his fiancée and leaving for some unknown destination, actions that would sever his financial supplies. The thought of losing his sources of money has a very bad effect on his nerves, and he tries to think of some way of keeping on with the Baron.

The narrator, who feels contempt for Morel, is at this moment thinking of breaking off with Albertine, who has been far more deeply compromised by him than Jupien's niece by Morel. But art is on his mind as well, and the evening's entertainment will restore his faith in the reality of art, while taking away from him the calm he needs to practice it.

Swann, like Bergotte, has recently died. The narrator muses that Swann's death is more of a death than Bergotte's, because all Swann's artistic discrimination had gone into his conversation. At any rate, the narrator misses Swann's conversation, for there are so many questions he would like to ask him. But even if Swann risks being forgotten, the narrator himself will have done something to preserve his memory, by putting him into one of his books.

The narrator asks Brichot, whom he has met on his way to the Verdurins and whose sight is almost extinct, if it was at the Verdurins' present residence that Swann had met his future wife but Brichot replies that at that time the Verdurins lived in a different building. Brichot tells him about those former times, which seem enchanting to the narrator. The narrator particularly regrets not having paid more attention to Swann.

Then the Baron de Charlus approaches, closely followed by one of those underworld characters who have recently begun to attach themselves to him. He looks and sounds far more obviously homosexual than he had done when the narrator first met him at Balbec. Now the narrator informs us that homosexuality in the time of the Greeks was a matter of fashion, while the modern kind is a neurosis that one cannot control or conceal. He also reveals that homosexuals have a much more acute sensibility concerning artistic matters than heterosexuals do. Since the function of the Baron this evening is to present a grand concert in which Morel will star, this reflexion is very much to the point.

The narrator is so struck by the Baron's taste in artistic matters that he is sorry that the Baron has never written books. His creativity has been limited to such things as painting a fan for Oriane and accompanying Morel on the piano. The spiritual essence he would have put into his books would have made him much more likable. His amazingly rich vocabulary would also have been useful. But perhaps, after all, he might not have been able to put his talent in his writing.

The Baron is in a very good mood. He would not be in such a good mood if he knew of the scene Morel had with his fiancée, but Jupien has not informed him of it. He lavishes advice on the narrator as to how Albertine should dress—advice to which the narrator listens attentively. He also jokes with the narrator and Brichot about their intimacy, in a very "chichi" way, as if they were homosexual too. His mask, so rigorously maintained for so long, is slipping badly as a result of relaxing in the Verdurin circle. He has acquired the habit of talking about homosexuality all the time, as if it were an entertaining topic. But he still feels it necessary to be discreet—in his fashion—about his relations with Morel. He claims that there is nothing but friendship between him and Morel and remarks that he knows nothing of Morel's life. Probably he is ignorant about much of Morel's life or he would not have been so completely consternated by a love letter from Léa to Morel in which Morel is addressed in the feminine. Inversion inverted becomes less heterosexual rather than more so, according to Proust. If the Baron had been a writer like Bergotte, the narrator remarks, he could have benefited from this surprise.

As the three approach the Verdurin residence, the Baron inquires after Bloch, who keeps on reentering the narrator's life after having apparently left it forever. The Baron has Morel followed by detectives, but he is also interested in other young men, whom he tries to connect with Morel through their verse or musical compositions. However, what is chiefly on his mind at this particular moment is the concert in which Morel is to perform at the Verdurins that evening and for which the Baron has issued all the invitations himself. He has assembled an aristocratic audience because, he says, they will talk about the concert in the right places. At the same time, Bergotte (this is one of the inconsistencies Proust did not live to correct) should help Morel to get his little sketches published. (People tend to die and come to life again rather erratically in *La Prisonnière*, which was published but not in its final state when Proust himself died.) Another little job of Morel's is to publish libels for the Baron against the Comtesse Molé. These affect her so cruelly that she dies of chagrin. But Charlus will fall and Morel will rise.

Charlus, still on the subject of the narrator and Albertine, says it is a good thing the narrator did not bring her that evening, as Mlle Vinteuil and her friend are supposed to be there. However, since they did not attend the rehearsal in the afternoon, they may not come. Now the narrator understands why Albertine had wanted to visit Madame Verdurin that afternoon. He suddenly looks so ill that the Baron notices it. The narrator notes that he would be quite happy to let Albertine go wherever she likes provided he could lock up Mlle Vinteuil and her friend. Saniette joins them.

They enter the Verdurins' residence, where the Baron flirts with the servant who takes his coat. M. Verdurin comes to greet them and insults Saniette, before informing him, exactly like the Duc de Guermantes, that he is exaggerating because he has said that the Princesse Sherbatoff is dead. He and Mme Verdurin are determined to have their evening's entertainment, all the more so because they have made up their minds to make Morel break with the Baron de Charlus. They are annoyed with Morel for not wanting to play without the Baron, and they are even more annoyed with the Baron for inviting his friends to their reception and refusing to let them invite their own friends. This is particularly exasperating for Mme Verdurin as, after gaining public notice by getting a Dreyfusard salon together and patronizing the Russian ballet, she is beginning to attract the attention of certain aristocratic ladies whom the Baron insists on excluding.

When she hears that the Princesse Sherbatoff, the faithful of the faithful, has deserted her for death, Mme Verdurin proceeds to criticize her. She is prepared to feel intense emotion over the music of Vinteuil but not over the death of Princesse Sherbatoff. The same thing applies to Cottard, who is also dead (for the moment, like Bergotte, for he will reappear). Meanwhile, the narrator is preoccupied with the whereabouts of Mlle Vinteuil—egoism is universal—and Charlus discusses sexual possibilities with some eminent men, when he is not mingling with those he thinks of as *his* guests. The only one of these guests who pays proper attention to Mme Verdurin is the Queen of Naples.

However, Charlus does not allow his guests to be rude to Morel, and imposes silence on them for the concert. Indeed, he has every reason to demand silence, for what is being played is a previously unknown septet by Vinteuil. The narrator describes this piece of music with such consummate artistry, making use of colored audition, that we truly seem to hear this music we have never heard before as we have never heard any music before. Until the narrator's attention flags for a moment and he starts looking at Mme Verdurin to see how that high priestess of music is behaving, and then allows his thoughts to wander to Albertine, he is enraptured by the music and far above all the dreary preoccupations that have been besetting him. It is a glimpse of heaven in the midst of hell, for joy is what dominates the conclusion, where the narrator is lifted to the heights. Now the narrator is convinced that art is real, and not only real but the true, the more abundant life. The great creators come from another world, as Proust had suggested in his passage on the death of Bergotte, and give us glimpses of that supernatural home. Nothing less can serve as communication of our essential nature or be truly worthy of our love. And the narrator applies this to his own experiences, with a certain hope.

His soul enlarged by the music of Vinteuil, the narrator is willing to acknowledge a debt of gratitude to Mlle Vinteuil's friend, who has used her musical knowledge and ability to decipher the rough jottings Vinteuil left behind, and to extend a pardon to Mlle Vinteuil. These later works of Vinteuil he compares to the later works of Wagner and Victor Hugo. Furthermore, if what the narrator calls vice had a part to play in preserving these later works of Vinteuil, vice, in the persons of Charlus and Morel, also helped to make these works accessible to the public.

Everyday life resumes: M. Verdurin throws Saniette out of the house for speaking old-fashioned French; Saniette has an attack in the courtyard and has to be carried home; Ski plays the piano and the fool; and M. de Charlus accepts the thanks of "his" guests as if they had no reason to thank the Verdurins. At the same time he makes offensive remarks about the Verdurins in which his guests join. In his element as an acknowledged leader of society, he bullies certain of his guests into agreeing to invite Morel to play at their own receptions. M. de Charlus, congratulating Mme Verdurin afterward on the success of the evening, is as jubilant as Mme Verdurin is furious. Perhaps the most annoying feature of the evening, for her, is that Morel has been invited to play outside her salon, and her husband will be invited to hear him, but she will not be invited.

Completely unconscious of Mme Verdurin's fury, the Baron pulls strings to be sure that Morel will be awarded the Cross of the Legion of Honor which he has done nothing to deserve. While his back is turned, Mme Verdurin instructs Brichot to occupy the Baron's attention, allowing her husband to take Morel to one side and warn him of the mortal danger he runs in associating with the Baron. Like Françoise exclaiming "sale bête" (filthy beast) over the chicken she has killed, Mme Verdurin justifies the execution she is planning by uttering a series of slanders. Brichot, gratefully remembering how Mme Verdurin had put a stop to his affair with his laundress, but uneasy in his conscience that M. de Charlus will be very unhappy at being separated from Morel, obeys Mme Verdurin's order, and the narrator accompanies him and M. de Charlus to the smoking room.

What M. de Charlus most wants to talk about is Morel, and, in particular, the moment when a lock of hair fell over the musician's forehead. The narrator has his own preoccupations, and questions the Baron about Mlle Vinteuil, but without receiving an answer. Brichot goes to fetch a coat to put over the narrator, and the Baron praises Brichot, whose courses he sometimes attends, without realizing that Brichot stabs him in the back. The conversation turns to Mme de Villeparisis (another character who is temporarily dead). Brichot comes back and leads the Baron to give a lecture on the history and sociology of homosexuality, to which Brichot also contributes, taking a malicious pleasure in this diversion.

When sufficient time has elapsed, Brichot leads the Baron and the narrator toward Mme Verdurin, who has been informing Morel, with the aid of her husband, that he has a very bad reputation at the Conservatoire—which is the fate Morel most dreads—because of his association with the Baron de Charlus, and that the Baron is planning to make a fool of him by claiming that he will receive the Cross of the Legion of Honor. She also forbids him to play for any of the aristocratic ladies who came that evening, for that would make him seem like a dilettante.

The narrator is on tenterhooks at the idea of the scene that is about to happen, and his only consolation is that the Baron de Charlus will fly into one of his magnificent rages and pulverize his would-be tormenters. In actual fact, when Morel rejects and disowns him, with the utmost violence, just when the Baron was expecting joy and gratitude for news of the Cross of the Legion of Honor, the latter receives such a shock that he is completely helpless. It takes the strength of character of the Queen of Naples, who has come back to look for her fan, to lead M. de Charlus out of this den of bandits into which he has strayed.

M. de Charlus takes no revenge against the Verdurins because he comes down with pneumonia and hovers close to death. His eloquence has become entirely Christian, and he pleads with the Archangel Gabriel to announce the coming of the Messiah, meaning Morel, or with the Archangel Raphael to bring Morel back like the young Tobias. He suggests that if Brichot brings him back, his sight will be restored. But as M. de Charlus gets better, he becomes less Christian.

The focus switches suddenly to the Verdurins, who are discussing how to support Saniette in his poverty without letting him know that the money comes from them. They put Cottard in charge of making proper arrangements. Flashes of goodness can illuminate even the basest human nature, the narrator concludes, but he is even more struck by how contradictory human nature always is. Brichot's malicious way of talking about M. de Charlus, whom he believes he likes, as he accompanies the narrator to his home, is another example of this contradiction.

Then the narrator is once more absorbed by Albertine, who is completely exasperated by his jealous spying when he says he has just been to visit the Verdurins. They have a quarrel about it, in which Albertine reveals that the focal point of the evening, for her, would have been Mlle Vinteuil. The narrator, hurling his darts more or less at random, says first that she had not told him that she had met Mlle Vinteuil the other day, then that she had been hiding things from him about her trip to Balbec. The second dart hits home. Albertine confesses that she and the chauffeur just pretended to go to Balbec and that she had someone else mail the postcards supposedly marking their trip. Then the narrator gets back to Mlle Vinteuil. To his amazement, Albertine confesses that she had told him a lie when she said she had been practically brought up by Mlle Vinteuil and her friend. She had told him this simply to make herself sound important. But she does admit to knowing Mlle Vinteuil's friend slightly. She imagines that Mlle Vinteuil's friend has told the narrator that she does not know her because she despises her.

Touched by Albertine's modesty, the narrator offers her money to dress up and encourages her to invite M. and Mme Verdurin to dinner. Albertine mutters in a tone of contempt that she does not want to invite those old people and she would much sooner the narrator left her free to go and get herself. . . . ("se faire casser" . . . She stops there and looks extremely embarrassed. The narrator ponders the unspoken word or words, which she refuses to supply, and comes up with something he considers unspeakable. The missing words he supplies are "le pot" (buggered) (*La Prisonnière*, 447).[3] (This passage is omitted in the English translations.) For a moment he goes into shock. To gain time, he proposes an immediate separation, to which he is pretty sure that Albertine will not consent.

They keep up this game of the fake separation, with Albertine protesting that he is the only one she loves, and incidentally revealing that she has given her photograph to Bloch's cousin Esther. The narrator has the leisure to meditate on the act he is putting on, and concludes that if there is so little real understanding between any two people under ordinary circumstances, it is a thousand times worse in a love relationship, which is bound to be manipulative. Paradoxically, because Albertine really wants her freedom, she feels obliged to protest against the idea of a separation, and because the narrator wants her to have no freedom at all, he insists on it. The narrator knows perfectly well that, whether she is guilty or innocent, she must be thoroughly tired of being restricted and spied on all the time, and consequently cannot possibly enjoy his company as much as she claims to do. So he has to bluff.

Acting as plaintiff, prosecuting counsel, judge, and jury, the narrator continues to interrogate Albertine. She admits that she lied when she said that Andrée was attracted to Bloch. She had lied only so that the narrator would not have his doubts about her. And she had lied when she claimed not to know Léa, because she had taken a three-week trip with her. The narrator concludes that Albertine only tells him the truth when she thinks he knows it already. He knows she must be concealing countless other lies. But he admits for the first time that the lies he tells her put them on an equal footing.

After pushing the threat of a separation as far as possible, in order to force Albertine to say that she is happy with him, the narrator pretends to change his mind. Albertine tries to placate him by arranging to have witnesses to her every act. Meanwhile the narrator makes inquiries behind her back, while Françoise, who hates Albertine as much as she had hated Eulalie, also spies on her, of her own accord, in the hope of bringing about her downfall. The narrator begins to be seriously worried that Albertine will actually want a separation. At the same time, he is much calmer now that Albertine is being so well behaved, and thinks of pretty things to give her to make her prison more attractive, such as the old silver he had intended to put in the yacht he had once thought of giving her. He also gives her Fortuny gowns imitating the dresses of the sixteenth century (designed by the couturier Fortuny y Madrazo, who really existed). These gowns are rich, elaborate, and, above all, meant to be worn at home. The Albertine in constant movement from one beach to another no longer exists. These gowns are worn by a tedious slave.

The narrator gets Albertine to play the pianola for him. He particularly likes her to play music by Vinteuil, now that he no longer has any reason to be jealous of Mlle Vinteuil. Instead, he is more inclined to be jealous of Morel, whom Albertine had asked to meet, and Léa. But he takes great pleasure in following the structure of Vinteuil's music, which seems to him to be more true than any book, for musical themes are not distorted by thought processes. Life would have no meaning if the higher, purer, truer emotion one gets from a sculpture or a piece of music did not correspond to a certain spiritual reality. A beautiful phrase by Vinteuil reminds him of the special pleasure the narrator had derived from the madeleine, the steeples of Martinville, and certain trees along a road in Balbec.

He comments to Albertine that the individuality of Vinteuil's music is a sign of his genius. At her prompting, he proceeds to unveil examples of this new and beautiful individuality in literature, in the works of Barbey d'Aurevilly, Thomas Hardy, Stendhal, and Dostoyevsky, only pausing for a moment to question Albertine about her relations with Gilberte. Albertine encourages him to develop his literary ideas, but he prefers to get her to talk instead, for instance, about her visit to Amsterdam. His love for her extends so far in time and space that she is like a mighty Goddess of Time, and he need not regret having spent so much money on her because the suffering she has brought him has opened up to him the lives of other people.

This does not mean that his suffering ceases. For instance, Mme Bontemps, Albertine's aunt, reveals that Albertine and Andrée used to go every day to the Buttes-Chaumont, which Albertine had told the narrator she had never visited. She also reveals a more important fact: if Albertine had been ready to leave Balbec at a moment's notice with the narrator, it was because she had been expecting Andrée and had just learned that Andrée was unable to come. Thus Albertine had been able to kill two birds with one stone, according to her habit, and do what suited herself and Andrée as well as the narrator. But he decides not to talk about this discovery at the moment, in order to keep Albertine from being more eager to leave him than she already is. He is sure she will leave, but *he* wants to be able to decide when.

However, when she puts on a blue and gold Fortuny gown that makes him long to be in Venice, he gives way to a fit of anger and reproaches her for her ingratitude. Then he begs her pardon, and goes on to say that wicked people are trying to separate them. As an example, he brings up the subject of her relations with Mlle Vinteuil, which she denies. Then he turns to the subject of her relations with Andrée. She is furious, and wants to confront the people who have been gossiping about her, or so she says. Then he tells her that she left Balbec with him because Andrée was not coming. Albertine is so angry that she says she wants to have nothing more to do with Andrée.

That night Albertine refuses to kiss him. Although the narrator tries to reason himself into thinking that she cannot leave yet, he is deeply troubled. He has a kind of presentiment of her death. They stay together, at the narrator's request, until morning, and Albertine shows that she feels that the springtime is passing without her. Suddenly, back in her room, Albertine throws her window open, against all the rules the narrator has imposed. This throws him into a panic, and it is with deep anxiety that he checks on Albertine's whereabouts the following morning.

They go for a walk and see a plane, that symbol of freedom. Then they go into a pastry shop, where the narrator observes Albertine's futile attempts to attract the waitress. He recites poetry about the moon to her, but this attempt to capture her interest is a failure. They are obviously bored, and the narrator, as already mentioned, longs to set out for Venice, leaving Albertine behind. But he receives the most terrible shock when Françoise tells him, the following morning, that Albertine has gone. Compagnon comments that Albertine is innocently cruel, like a Racinian *ingénue* (183–84), but that the narrator is capable of more cruelty than anyone else in the book (175–76).

So this is the narrator's great love. It is even worse than his love for Gilberte, which he managed to get over fairly easily, and which was based in some way on feelings of friendship and reciprocity. He gave up Gilberte because he felt that she would never care for him as much as he cared for her, which was true enough, so there was something genuine about their relationship, at least in the ending of it. There was a certain distance between them, running contrary to the chains of habit. And he had a fairly clear idea of Gilberte's personality and interests, her position in society, and her home background. In other words, she, in herself, was not a problem, whereas Albertine is. The narrator is incapable of any degree of objectivity toward Albertine, because of his lust (more spiritual than physical) to contain and possess her. And the more difficult this is, the more he hungers for it. He was happy in being contained by his grandmother, but his attempts to contain Albertine are doomed to endless failure because she does not and cannot contain him.

Chapter Seven

La Fugitive (Albertine disparue) (The Fugitive)

Proust originally intended to give to this volume the title *La Fugitive*, but when he heard it was already taken, he substituted *Albertine disparue*. (The Flammarion edition keeps the title *La Fugitive*.) Nor is this the only thing Proust substituted. Shortly before his death he took one of the typescripts of *Albertine disparue* and made massive cuts in it, with the intent of making the narrator's anxiety and grief over the departure and death of Albertine briefer and more dramatic. The revised version leaves a considerable gap in the narrative between the period shortly following Albertine's death and the narrator's visit to Venice, with Albertine so completely dismissed from his mind that he can take a lively interest in the absurdities of M. de Norpois. But all the editions of *A La Recherche du temps perdu* favor the lengthier version that Proust's brother, Robert, submitted to Gallimard for publication after Proust's death. The short version was published separately in 1987 under the title *Albertine disparue* by Nathalie Mauriac, Robert Proust's great-granddaughter, and Etienne Wolff. In fact, the lengthier version gives a better idea of the narrator's struggle to get over Albertine. One must make a back-breaking effort to read it, but the original longer version rewards the reader's work with a faithful reflection of the narrator's effort to come to terms with his loss.

Another thing that comes out more clearly in the longer version is the extent to which Albertine exists in the narrator's mind rather than as a separate reality. This Proust makes very clear in the series of ruminations that encase the actual events, of which there are few. When Proust reduced the narrative to almost nothing but the events in the abridged manuscript, he cut the volume by half. There are times when, on reading *La Fugitive* as Robert Proust handed it down to us, we feel, as Leo Bersani observes, that we are reading maxims on the passions, of a type current in seventeenth-century France.[1] Although Proust confines direct reference to Pascal to his *foi expérimentale* (faith proved by experience), his method of demonstrating the futility of passion is very Pascalian. Perhaps this is what made Proust feel he was being too abstract.

La Fugitive begins where *La Prisonnière* left off, with the news of Albertine's departure. The narrator now realizes that he had been completely mistaken in wishing that Albertine would leave and in thinking that he would not miss her. The terrible suffering to which he succumbs on learning that she has gone tells him something different about himself and his true feelings, and he can only lessen his suffering by taking pity on himself as if he were someone else and telling himself that he will make her come back. It is Proust's plan, as I previously stated, to show the narrator making progress in self-knowledge. While enduring the terrible suffering that Albertine's departure evokes in him, he learns that it is not enough to trust to one's intelligence for self-knowledge, for intelligence leaves habit out of account, and Albertine's presence has become a habit for him. One might go further than Proust and say that it has become an addiction. The addict thinks it will be easy to give up his habit, until he actually begins to experience withdrawal and the agony that accompanies it.

This is only the beginning of the narrator's long struggle against pain and grief, for he goes on to read the farewell letter Albertine has left behind. Albertine says that their relationship had taken a turn for the worse and would shortly have become impossible, so she has decided to leave while they can still part as good friends. Her decision, she says, is final. The narrator immediately supposes that she is bluffing and trying to frighten him. He leaps to the conclusion that money is the answer to everything: that Mme Bontemps is conspiring with Albertine to get money out of him, that he therefore needs to bribe Mme Bontemps with half his fortune, that he will buy Albertine the Rolls Royce and the yacht he had half promised her, and that he will spend money on Albertine like water for seven or eight years, and then kill himself for lack of funds. If Albertine wants complete freedom, she will have it. Moreover, he will marry her. However, underlying these ideas is another one: Albertine really would be happier without him, as her attitudes and behavior before leaving him certainly made clear.

All the narrator really knows is that he is suffering more than he has ever suffered before, and his suffering is intensified by every familiar object around him, since everything real is associated with Albertine. His suffering is real, not the product of his imagination and his intelligence, and it is in league with everything else that is real. The way Albertine looked before her departure, her visible gloom, her window flung open in the night—these were all real and obviously had nothing to do with emotional blackmail designed to get money out of him. They were real, visible signs that Albertine had had enough of living with the narrator on his terms. He recognizes that it will not be easy to get her to come back, even though he still keeps on lying to himself, telling himself that she will be back that evening. He cannot give her up as he had given up Gilberte, but he is determined not to ask her to come back, for that would mean abandoning every scrap of the prestige he may still hold for her. In the meantime he avoids looking at her chair, her pianola, all the objects she had used. He feels as if he were composed of innumerable "I"'s that all have to learn in turn that Albertine has gone.

His only hope is that Albertine has gone to stay with her aunt in Touraine, while his worst fear is that she is in Paris or has gone to Amsterdam or Montjouvain. But as soon as the concierge tells him that she left for Touraine, which moments before had seemed the most preferable alternative because there Albertine's aunt would keep an eye on her, Touraine becomes the most terrible alternative, simply because it is a real and no longer merely a possible destination for Albertine.

Grief is his constant companion. He tries to shake it off by inviting a little girl in, cuddling her, and giving her a large sum of money. He does not seem to see anything odd in this behavior; indeed, he has done this kind of thing before. The girls the narrator is attracted to get younger and younger as he gets older. But even if this episode calms him for a moment, his grief soon returns, and he repeats Albertine's name to himself over and over again, as if he had been transformed into a bird and her name were his birdcall. Now the narrator concludes that the essential boon that the presence of the beloved bestows is nothing physical, but instead the cessation of anxiety. One even forgets what the beloved looks like, love is so subjective.

He has already decided that he cannot go in person to get Albertine to come back, so he has the bright idea of asking Saint-Loup to act as his emissary. This idea really cheers him up, for if Saint-Loup agrees to do it, the narrator will be able to go on lying to Albertine by assuming indifference about her flight and return. The essence of this little conspiracy is that Saint-Loup should appear to be acting on his own initiative, and should avoid being seen by Albertine, even though it will be completely obvious to one and all what is going on. The narrator recognizes a further complication: Saint-Loup could be offended that the narrator had been hiding things from him, since the narrator had never told him that he had been keeping Albertine under his roof all winter. But the narrator is beyond thinking of possible consequences. He sends for Saint-Loup and shows him Albertine's photograph. Saint-Loup is appalled to think that such a homely girl should cause the narrator so much suffering. The narrator and Saint-Loup have exchanged roles, for earlier the narrator had had the same thought concerning Saint-Loup and Rachel. However, Saint-Loup is quite willing to go through with the narrator's plan, although he does have doubts about Mme Bontemps accepting 30,000 francs for her husband's electoral campaign. Saint-Loup is an indomitable friend, and leaves immediately, ready for anything.

Bloch turns up soon afterward and tells the narrator that he had begged Mme Bontemps to tell Albertine to be nicer to the narrator. The narrator is furious because he has the fixed idea that Albertine will be more likely to love him if he never shows how much he cares for her. One trouble follows another, for the narrator is now haled before the police by the parents of the little girl he cuddled. Fortunately, the police inspector who hears the parents' complaint is himself a child molester. Once the parents leave, the inspector gives the narrator advice on better ways to practice his deviancy. The narrator goes home in a very confused state but immediately reverts to thoughts of Albertine. He is joyful in his assurance that Saint-Loup will shortly return, bringing her with him, although it is hard for him to go on believing this when he rereads Albertine's farewell letter. Then he is dragged back to thoughts of his recent mishap because Françoise says that a police inspector has been asking the concierge if the narrator often brings girls home, and the concierge had said yes. The narrator thinks the building is being watched by the police.

As a result, the narrator realizes that he can never again bring home another child to console him, and life seems without value to him as a result. Here again we have an example of the things the narrator does not know about himself and that he is discovering in his agony. But this episode also underlines the state of extreme confusion he is in, because he suddenly thinks that he must have been a child molester in keeping Albertine, even though Albertine is no child. The French would say "Il a perdu le nord" (He doesn't know which end is up). He is so upset by the thought that he will be visited by the police and the fear that the returned Albertine will witness his humiliation, that he becomes horrified by the idea of her return, and would like to telegraph her not to come back. He cannot stand the idea of being diminished in her eyes. And then immediately he switches round and passionately wants her to come back.

After that he has moments of calm and even daydreams again of Venice and beautiful women. When he realizes that he has been daydreaming he is terrified, for he sees in this reverie the beginning of forgetfulness, which means the death of what he is now. Forgetfulness equals oblivion. But this state of mind is only momentary, while he dreams of Albertine every night. All forgetfulness does, for the time being, is idealize Albertine. When some object belonging to her reminds him of her, he nearly faints. To go to bed without her goodnight kiss makes him suffer as he had suffered as a child in the *drame du coucher*. But as time draws out, he is able to keep on living without her. Not that he thinks for one moment of accepting a proposal of marriage that he receives from a niece of the Duc de Guermantes. He is not even flattered by this proposal because it would not have made him seem more important to Albertine. He can only wish for her to return, whether he receives her in joy or anger. But all this only goes to show that Albertine exists solely in his mind. Furthermore, the narrator maintains that, in similar circumstances, this is the case for everybody.

The narrator finally receives a telegram from Robert de Saint-Loup in which he says that Albertine has seen him at her aunt's house and her discovery has ruined the whole plan. The narrator is furious. Then he weeps on hearing airs from *Manon* from upstairs, for he identifies himself with Des Grieux and Albertine with Manon. Albertine sends him a telegram, reproaching him for sending Saint-Loup to her aunt and asking why he had not approached her directly, for she would have been glad to return. His spirits rise, but almost immediately he decides not to rush things. He writes back, mendaciously as always, saying they should not be in a hurry to see each other again and she had made the right decision in leaving. At the same time he slips in the news that he had received his mother's consent to their marriage and that he had set about buying a yacht and a Rolls Royce for her, and would have had verses by Mallarmé engraved on them. She could do him a service by canceling the order. As for Saint-Loup, the narrator claims to know nothing about his mission.

We see how autobiographical *La Fugitive* is when we compare this letter to the one that Proust wrote to Alfred Agostinelli, offering him an airplane, and which Agostinelli never received because he died in a flying accident first.[2] But Albertine's death does not follow immediately on this letter. For the time being the narrator is tied in knots, as he envisages Albertine's possible responses. He is so divided that he regrets giving the letter to Françoise to mail, but when she brings it back to ask how many stamps she should put on it, he gives it to her again. On reading news of the death of Berma, he compares his divided feelings to those of Phèdre in her declaration to Hippolyte. This is the first reference to Racine in *A La Recherche du temps perdu* not intended to be funny. But the narrator's allusion to Racine reflects a very personal and very peculiar interpretation of Racine, because he sees Phèdre as behaving like himself, rather than himself behaving like Phèdre, while Albertine is compared to Hippolyte. But certainly the comparison carries with it the intuition that he is driving Albertine to her death, and even of the kind of death he is driving her to.

A little later, the narrator gets a very unpleasant shock when Françoise points out to him that Albertine has left her rings behind, and notes that they must have been given to her by the same person, because the workmanship is the same. (Albertine had claimed that she had received one from her aunt and had bought the other.) He takes this observation as new evidence of betrayal, and his mind is full from then on of thoughts of betrayal, which are not, however, accompanied by images of Albertine. Then he receives a letter from Albertine thanking him for his letter and saying she is quite ready to countermand the order for the Rolls. She has very pretty things to say about their last walk together (here Proust apparently makes use of the last letter he received from Agostinelli). But she appears to have no intention of returning. He writes back, in their usual vein of emotional blackmail, to say that he is thinking of asking Andrée to come and live with him and notes that he is even thinking of asking her to marry him, since her temperament accords better with his than Albertine's could ever have done.

He is obviously working to arouse her jealousy, but he has a dreadful doubt after sending off this letter that this particular stratagem will not work. He suffers at this idea, but not nearly as much as he suffers when Saint-Loup returns. Waiting for Saint-Loup in the stairwell, he overhears him advising a Guermantes servant about how to get one of the other servants dismissed. A mean, spiteful Saint-Loup appears, quite different from the one the narrator thought he knew. His confidence in him is shaken, and he blames him bitterly for the failure of his mission. Saint-Loup is understandably vexed. In particular, they have an absurd quarrel about how Saint-Loup had failed, or not failed, in getting Mme Bontemps to accept the narrator's bribe.

The narrator shows himself to be petty, childish, and unreasonable. His fears of what Albertine may be doing with the girls and young women Saint-Loup encountered in and around Mme Bontemps's house enter into this quarrelsome mood. He starts feeling that he would do better to go and get Albertine himself. He even starts wishing, as Swann had done with Odette, that she were dead, so that he could recover his peace of mind. (We know from past experience what happens when the narrator wishes things.) The narrator is so beside himself that he sends Albertine a desperate telegram begging her to come back immediately on any conditions. But then he receives a telegram from Mme Bontemps, informing him that Albertine is dead as the result of a riding accident, presumably in Touraine. (The abridged typescript says she died by the banks of the Vivonne, confirming the narrator's suspicion that she had joined Mlle Vinteuil and her friend. Much critical interest has been aroused by this change.) Then two letters arrive from Albertine. One says that she would be delighted for Andrée to live with him. The other proposes a prompt return.

Now the narrator has to live with countless memories of the living Albertine. She is not, cannot be, dead for him. A ray of sunlight makes him think of a church they looked at together. The cider and cherries Françoise brings him make him think of the Norman farms they visited together. He is reminded of her by sunsets; he is horrified by the idea of walking in a forest, because she has thrown against a tree, but open country reminds him of her too; fog reminds him of her; moonlight reminds him of her; stars remind him of her; the dawn reminds him of her. He had thought that Albertine prevented him from going to Venice, but now he would rather not go. Autumn and winter will bring no solace, because they too are associated with Albertine.

In other words, for some time to come, Albertine will live within him, recalled by every change of time and season. His jealousy lives on after the demise of its object, and he hits on the idea of asking Aimé, the maître d'hôtel he had met in Balbec, to conduct an inquiry into Albertine's behavior at Balbec. But before hearing from Aimé, he spends page after page brooding on the past. Many of his memories of her are very sweet. He is angry with the Verdurins because Albertine has died so young and Brichot is still going to dinner with them. He feels completely empty without her. He feels personally responsible for her death. But we see his pain gradually changing to a sweet regret as he thinks about the many accidental things that led to his meeting with Albertine. He notes that Mme de Stermaria could have been the great love of his life. Gilberte and Albertine had something in common that attracted him, it is true, but if he had not gone to Balbec he would never have met Albertine. And if he had not brought Albertine to live with him, he would never have forged the chains that bound them together. Or he could have loved Andrée. At any rate, he is happy that Albertine should have written to him in loving terms before she died. He even gets to the point of thinking that if she had admitted she was lesbian, he would have accepted it and she would still be alive.

He daydreams of a reunion in heaven, a reunion that would still be physical, or of a letter from her saying that she is not dead. Although he knows she is dead, he hopes to see her walk in at any minute. All this is almost pleasant, but then he is galvanized into his old jealousy by a letter from Aimé, in which he says that the bathhouse attendant at Balbec considered Albertine a lesbian because she came so often and stayed so long with other girls and women. Immediately he suffers worse than he has ever suffered before; Balbec seems like a hell to him, Albertine's lesbianism horrifies him so much.

Absurdly, he wants to be able to tell Albertine, who no longer exists, that he knows about her activities. He had not really believed that Albertine was lesbian until he got this letter, even though he thought he did, and also thought that everything would have been all right if she had confessed to him. (There are a lot of contradictions here, but it is typical of the narrator's confused state of mind that his ideas should be contradictory.) Finally he seeks refuge in his grandmother's statement that the bathhouse attendant was a born liar. But this thought does not console him for long, because the violence of the shock he has received has brought his anguish to a state of paroxysm.

Then he has the idea of sending Aimé to make inquiries near Mme Bontemps's house at Nice (a flagrant reference to Agostinelli that appears in the Flammarion edition, but we read "Touraine" in the new Pléiade edition). Aimé soon replies that he has located a little laundress who used to engage in erotic games with Albertine by the water's edge (either on the beaches of the Mediterranean or the banks of the Loire, for Proust seems to have found it hard to decide), to Albertine's intense delight. Aimé has painted this picture so clearly, in a few simple words, that it is of pictures that the narrator now thinks. He thinks of a painting by Elstir of girls sporting by the water's edge, which seems based on Les Grandes Baigneuses by Renoir, and then of a study of Leda and the Swan, because the curve of Albertine's leg used to make him think of a swan's neck. J. E. Rivers has some very interesting comments on the narrator's ideas about this picture, in which he analyzes the narrator's obsessive imagination at work.[3] He longs to be able to tell Albertine that he knows about her lesbian identity.

Gradually his love for Albertine begins to fade away. But it does not disappear all at once, because just as he sees Albertine split into multiple personalities, so he himself is split into multiple personalities, some of which remember her more vividly than others. And the whole sequence of memories has become very uneven and irregular. Habit will destroy these thoughts of Albertine altogether, in the long run. His dreams show that his preoccupation with Albertine is only partial. He has finally realized that she no longer exists, even though painful thoughts of her come to the surface from time to time. Then Andrée comes to see him, and the narrator sees in her the incarnate desire of Albertine. He gets her to admit that she is lesbian, which makes him think that Albertine would have admitted it as readily to someone else, and he asks her to make love to one of the other members of the *petite bande* in front of him. Quite naturally, she refuses. She even says that no other member of the *petite bande* is a lesbian, and states that she never made love to Albertine.

This statement calms the narrator, but he still wants to know what lesbian love is like, so he gets two young laundresses to make love to each other in front of him. He finds a certain charm in this experiment, rather than suffering. New loves begin to seem possible for him, provided the women who appeal to him remind him in some way of Albertine. But every girl or woman he sees ends up disappointing him, even though he knows that the day will come when Albertine, like Gilberte earlier, will no longer mean anything to him. For the time being, thoughts of her are sweet, whereas it was the pain of his love that had proved its reality, and these thoughts incite him to follow the girls or young women he sees on his walks.

One day he is attracted by a group of three girls, one of whom turns and smiles at him. He is able to track them down as visitors to the Duchesse de Guermantes. The name of one of them, a blonde, is given to him as Mlle d'Eporcheville, whom he identifies as the girl Saint-Loup had told him frequented brothels. He sends a telegram to Saint-Loup to check his accuracy, and is informed in return that the name of the girl Saint-Loup has been talking about was de l'Orgeville, and that she was a chubby brunette. So the narrator decides to stop getting excited about the girl he saw.

Just when he has stopped being concerned about getting published, his article, to the pride and joy of his mother and himself, appears in *Le Figaro*. He tries to imagine how his readers will react, and hurries over to call on the Guermantes to find out what the Duc and Duchesse have to say about it. The girl he saw in the street, and whom he now feels he recognizes, is introduced to him as Mlle de Forcheville. She is now revealed to be his old friend Gilberte, for Odette had married

M. de Forcheville after Swann's death. The Duchesse de Guermantes had formerly refused to meet Mme and Mlle Swann, but after Swann's death she had changed her mind. Gilberte is trying to forget that she was ever anything but the daughter of Forcheville, an attempt in which she has the full support of the Guermanteses. Moreover, Gilberte is now an heiress, and aristocratic mothers are fighting over her as a good match for their sons. As for the article in *Le Figaro*, neither the Duc nor the Duchesse had noticed it. Out of goodwill, the Duc proceeds to read it, although he is not particularly complimentary about it. The Duchesse pretends interest, but does not read it. So much for the narrator's avid audience! However, the Duchesse invites him to the Opéra-Comique. He refuses, alleging his recent loss. From then on he proceeds to tell people about his grief, which he no longer feels.

Swann had hoped that his memory would be kept green by his daughter, but she has done her best to forget him. She has also helped the narrator to forget Albertine, which leads him to meditate on lapses of memory. Andrée hastens the work of forgetfulness when she comes to visit the narrator on his mother's day to be at home. M. de Charlus and Morel also come to visit him, M. de Charlus betraying his presence by reciting love poetry to Morel, but the narrator does not stay with them long. He is anxious to question Andrée, for he is still curious about Albertine even though he no longer loves her. Now Andrée admits quite readily that she had a physical relationship with Albertine, and adds that Albertine had got together with Morel to debauch innocent girls. They had even taken one to a brothel. Albertine had felt remorse afterward, and had restrained herself as long as she was with the narrator, but started such activities again as soon as she left him. It is quite possible that her riding accident was not an accident but a suicide, arising out of remorse.

Andrée goes on to reveal that she and Albertine had taken the risk of making love one day when the narrator and Françoise were out. When the narrator returned unexpectedly, they had concealed their state of confusion by saying that the smell of syringa made them ill. Albertine had been terrified that the narrator would realize what had been going on, for she was afraid of him and said at times that he was devious, spiteful, and hated her. But in fact he had no suspicions. The narrator comments that this revelation does not have the effect on him that it would have had formerly. However, he is not entirely certain that it is not a lie.

Andrée gets very angry at times, as with a young man she had known at Balbec, and then she does not care what she says. This does not prevent her from marrying the young man later on. She had been angry with him because she thought he did not care for her. But another surprise, which strikes the narrator more, is that the young man in question, who had seemed completely involved in material things, has produced a little play with scenery and costumes he had designed himself and which revealed him as a genius. (Proust is apparently thinking of Jean Cocteau.)

Getting back to Andrée's visit, Andrée reveals that the chief reason why Albertine had left the narrator was that she was afraid of what the other girls of the *petite bande* would think of her. She also reveals where she and Albertine liked to go to make love. The narrator thinks that probably the first impression he had had of Albertine had been correct. It was probably because Albertine was lesbian that she had seemed so frank and direct, like a good male friend.

Andrée pays him a further visit. This time she says that Mme Bontemps's pressure had induced Albertine to leave the narrator, because her aunt wanted to arrange a marriage between her and the young man from Balbec. When Albertine had wanted to visit Mme Verdurin, it had been to meet the young man in question, who was Mme Verdurin's nephew. Meditating on these revelations, the narrator tells himself that Albertine had been a victim. Andrée also says that there had never been anything physical between Albertine and Mlle Vinteuil and her friend. She adds that since Albertine recovered from typhoid fever she was in the habit of yielding to sudden inexplicable impulses. All this causes the narrator very little grief.

The narrator visits Venice with his mother. There he feels that he has become completely indifferent to Albertine. Venice, in his description, is a vision of delight, where all the smallest things are artistic and worthy of being put in a museum. At the same time, there is something so simple, familiar, and domestic about Venice that it makes him think of Combray. He goes in pursuit of Venetian girls and women, and follows them through endless little branches of the main canal. He is more in love with Venice than with the girls and women who live there.

Then he sees Mme de Villeparisis and M. de Norpois in a restaurant. The two old lovers have long outlived their love and are only bound together by habit. They may be intended to serve, although the narrator does not say so, as a kind of death's-head mockery of what he and Albertine might have become in the end—impossible to detach from one another, but reduced to conversing about trivial things. M. de Norpois is angry because he is no longer appreciated in diplomatic circles, and occasionally works off his anger on Mme de Villeparisis when he thinks she is being stupid.

Mme Sazerat is with his mother when the narrator returns to their table and mentions that he has seen Mme de Villeparisis. Mme Sazerat wants to see this woman who was so beautiful and for whom her father met financial ruin, but is unable to see any beauty in her. Vanity of vanities! Everything passes, everything wearies, and everything breaks, as the French say. It is hopeless to wish to see in the present what was real in the past. Mme de Villeparisis now and the Duchesse d'Havré, as she was then, are simply not the same person. Most of us outlive ourselves, unless we die young. Time is constantly at work, changing us and consequently changing the social kaleidoscope. Mme Sazerat can never see the woman who ruined her father, because she no longer exists. The multiple selves the narrator has experienced in his waning love for Albertine are part of everyone's fundamental nature. In the course of time many of these selves disappear for good, just as our appearance changes with age.

However, these changes are irregular and take place more rapidly in some people than others. M. de Norpois is not old enough to have given up his ambitions: he hopes by a striking intervention in Italian politics to obtain what he wants, which is a mission to the kaiser, followed by the post of ambassador to Constantinople. Consequently, when Prince Foggi joins them at their table, he seizes the opportunity to intervene in the composition of the Roman cabinet, to the outrage of M. Barrère, the French ambassador in Rome. However pleased M. de Norpois may be with his own political efficacy, to the narrator he is and always has been a joke. As his communiqués just before the war of 1870 indicate, his diplomacy is generally a purely cosmetic affair.

Even though the narrator has recovered sufficiently to enjoy the conversation of Mme de Villeparisis and M. de Norpois, the ghost of Albertine sometimes haunts him. He is reminded of her by a letter from his stockbroker about some rash investments he made when he was trying to make more money to spend on Albertine. His speculations have done so badly that he decides to sell all his stocks, after which he has only a fifth of what he had inherited from his grandmother. People in Combray think he has lost his money as a result of frequenting the aristocracy, which is far from the truth.

He is vexed to have lost so much money because he has taken a fancy to a young glass-seller whose complexion makes him think of a Titian and whom he would like to take with him to Paris. An expression in the stockbroker's letter makes him think for a moment of Albertine, but only for a moment. A stylized eagle he sees in San Giorgio dei Schiavoni makes him think of the eagles on Albertine's rings. But then a much more remarkable event happens, something that should have brought his love for Albertine back to life but does not. He receives a telegram in which the address is so distorted that the telegraph boy is not sure whether it is for him. The message runs: "Dear friend, you think I'm dead, pardon me, I am very much alive, I would like to see you, discuss marriage, when are you coming back? Love, Albertine." This telegram causes him no joy, and he is forced to recognize that he has changed as much as if his hair had turned white. The self that loved Albertine has been replaced. He cannot bring Albertine back to life in his emotions because he cannot bring his old self back to life. Forgetfulness, as he foresaw, has devoured his love.

He even wonders whether the news of Albertine's death had not roused his love to a pitch that it would not otherwise have reached and whether it would not have died a natural death otherwise. He tries to remember her, and what he remembers is a fat, mannish-looking woman whose profile is potentially that of Mme Bontemps. What she might have done with Andrée or others no longer interests him. His jealousy was an illness cured by time. And if he had married Albertine, how could he give any money to his new flame? He ends up telling the porter that the telegram was not intended for him. The porter does not want to take it back now that it has been opened, but the narrator is determined to act as if he had never received it. Like his love for Gilberte, his love for Albertine has been forgotten. He reflects that his love for himself, his desire to survive, will be destroyed by death in the same way.

That is almost the last thing he has to say about Albertine. She will be mentioned again, but in passing, in connection with the narrator's visits, in the company of his mother, to Saint Mark's and to the paintings of Carpaccio. He is viewing St. Mark's in connection with a study he is preparing on Ruskin. (Proust himself, of course, was a student of Ruskin.) Albertine had talked at Balbec of the pleasure it would give her to see certain paintings with him, and he had refused to believe that such a pleasure exists, but he now knows how much pleasure it gives him to have seen the art treasures of Venice with his mother. Then he goes on to say that on seeing *The Patriarch of Grado Exorcising a Possessed Man* he was struck by the fact that one of the characters in the painting is wearing a cloak identical to the one Albertine had worn to visit Versailles with the narrator shortly before her departure. The designer Fortuny must have copied it from Carpaccio. But the narrator's emotion is soon over, and he is completely devoted for the time being to artistic impressions, as simply happy as he had been in Combray.

The narrator and his mother take a trip to Padua to visit the Chapel of the Arena, painted with frescoes by Giotto. This trip revives and completes a memory of Combray, for Swann had given the boy photographs of the Vices and Virtues of Padua, but not the scenes of the life of the Virgin and of Christ. The little angels that appear in these frescoes seem as literally real in their actions as the Vices and Virtues had seemed to him in the past, for they are definitely flying creatures, like aviators, not human figures with wings attached. Again we see how the idea of the aviator and the airplane is suffused for Proust with tenderness.

Back at the hotel, the narrator takes an interest in a young Austrian woman who reminds him of Albertine. He would like to know if she too is lesbian, but there is no way of finding out; in any case she will shortly return to Austria. This episode does not probe very deep, but it does indicate that the narrator will always find a particular type of woman attractive. The type, rather than the individual, is what really matters to him, for he is so excited to find that Mme de Putbus with her servants is staying in their hotel that he decides to stay on in Venice, even though his mother had decided to leave and had sent their suitcases to the station. He remains behind when she has left for the station, listening to a musician singing "Sole mio." As he hesitates between staying and leaving, his anxiety becomes more and more intense until finally he rushes after his mother and joins her in the train, just as it is about to leave. Without his mother Venice has lost all its charm, and not even the prospect of finally falling into the arms of the Baronne de Putbus's chambermaid can hold him.

Once in the train, the narrator's thoughts are turned in another direction by a letter he had received from Gilberte shortly before leaving. It informs him of her marriage to Robert de Saint-Loup and expresses surprise at having had no reply to the telegram she had sent him. He suddenly realizes that the telegram he had received signed "Albertine" was actually from Gilberte, and explains exactly how the mistake could have occurred: Gilbert's ornate signature must have been mistaken for "Albertine" by the telegraph operator. His mother says that the news of Gilberte's marriage must be in one of the two letters she has received, for she had recognized that one was addressed in Robert de Saint-Loup's handwriting. But the one she has already read is far more surprising, for it announces the marriage of the young Cambremer with Mlle d'Oloron,

Jupien's niece, whom the Baron de Charlus has adopted and on whom he has bestowed one of the family titles. The narrator's mother says "C'est la récompense de la vertu. C'est un mariage à la fin d'un roman de Mme Sand" (It is the reward of virtue. It is the kind of wedding you find at the end of a novel by Mme Sand). The narrator thinks, "C'est le prix du vice, c'est un mariage à la fin d'un roman de Balzac" (It is the reward of vice. It is the kind of wedding you find at the end of a novel by Balzac).[4] The two of them discuss this marriage at considerable length, and the narrator's mother constantly comes back to the topic of what her mother would have thought of it. She is torn between regret that her mother had to remain ignorant of such an astonishing thing and relief that she has remained ignorant of something that would have shocked her.

Then the narrator informs us fully of all the intrigues that had taken place to bring about the marriage of Gilberte with Robert de Saint-Loup. This marriage has excited a great deal of comment in very different classes of society, even in the brothel of Maineville, where it is rumored that Saint-Loup and Cambremer are both homosexual. It seems that this rumor is the truth. But we will hear more about this subject later. For the time being, the narrator is chiefly concerned with the social upheavals these two marriages bring about—social upheavals which are, however, transitory. Both the young Cambremer and Gilberte, feeling that they have attained heights dizzier than they could have believed possible, lose interest in maintaining their social position. Robert de Saint-Loup is only too happy to go along with his wife's lack of interest in society. But poor Mlle d'Oloron dies of typhoid fever shortly after her marriage, so she is in no position to influence her husband's activities. A lack of interest in social climbing also comes to characterize Legrandin, last seen calling on Mme de Villeparisis, after he has succeeded in getting himself called the Comte de Méséglise (a title to which he has no right). His homosexual activities leave him no time for society. However, the young Cambremer does frequent the Baron de Charlus.

The narrator becomes good friends with Gilberte, now that his love, which was an obstacle to their friendship, has disappeared. He goes to visit her in Tansonville, where she and Robert have taken up residence, after he has arranged for his latest love, about whom he has nothing more to say, to be guarded by a homosexual friend. Gilberte is unhappy, since Robert is deceiving her. She thinks he has other women, but in actual fact he is involved with Morel. Jupien is shocked to discover that Morel abandoned the uncle for the nephew, particularly as the Baron loves Robert like a son, and tried to break up Robert's marriage. Now the narrator understands Saint-Loup's interest in Albertine, although he claims that his own interest in her was based on entirely different reasons. But while Jupien considers Saint-Loup's conversion to homosexuality as something extraordinary and quite recent, Aimé notes that he was already like that in Balbec, for he nearly caused a scandal because of his interest in the elevator boy. The narrator, having seen Saint-Loup with Rachel, does not believe him. However, he does remember Saint-Loup saying that Morel was a bit like Rachel. Proust is suggesting that the similarity between the two had enabled Saint-Loup to make the transition to homosexual love.

Saint-Loup pays out large sums of money to Rachel, to Morel, and to his mother-in-law; the latter's role is to make Gilberte do what her husband wants. He uses Gilberte's own money for these gifts and bribes, and neglects her, while displaying so much admiration for other women that she believes he is keeping mistresses. Thus he behaves like his uncle. Saint-Loup's behavior saddens Gilberte, but it also saddens the narrator so much that he has to struggle not to weep over Saint-Loup's downfall and, above all, over how their friendship has been tarnished.

The main feature of the last few pages of this volume is an account of the walks the narrator and Gilberte take at night before their late dinner. (This episode serves as the beginning to *Le Temps retrouvé* in the old Pléiade edition.) Combray no longer seems poetic, and the Vivonne seems narrow and ugly. His lack of emotional response makes the narrator feel that his capacity for feeling and imagining has diminished. But he is astonished to learn that they can get to Guermantes from Méséglise. He had always supposed that Swann's way was incompatible with the Guermantes way, and yet Gilberte's marriage to Robert de Saint-Loup is the social equivalent of this physical connection. Another surprise is to learn from Gilberte that she had been inviting him when she made an obscene gesture to him, all those years ago. He reflects that the real Gilberte and the real Albertine were the ones who had revealed themselves at his first glance, and he had spoiled everything by his clumsiness.

Gilberte follows this up by saying that she had invited him again by the way she had looked at him in the street, in Paris. In between, she had not been able to love him, because he conducted such an inquisition about everything she did. (In the Flammarion edition he does not ask who was the young man he saw her with on the Champs-Elysées, because he no longer cares.) But he is struck by Gilberte's account of her infant sexuality and says that she was truly of the Méséglise way—that is, on the sexual side—and regrets his ignorance of the sexual opportunities there had been all around him in Combray. Now all Gilberte's thoughts are for Robert, not that the narrator would dream of an affair with her anymore. These revelations have come too late, along with the destruction of the old beliefs and values. We are led to expect a kind of *Twilight of the Gods*, and indeed that is what we do get for a while, in *Le Temps retrouvé*, but Proust has a surprise ending prepared for his faithful readers.

Chapter Eight

Le Temps retrouvé (Time Regained)

Proust claimed to have written the beginning and end of *A la recherche du temps perdu* at the same time, and this claim is true in a sense. But *Le Temps retrouvé* owes much to Proust's impressions of the First World War, for it offers a picture of growing decadence. Disorder in the moral and social realms already marked the end of *La Fugitive*, but this disorder will increase up to the moment when the narrator will decide to live for himself alone and for his work, not out of misanthropy but because he has finally discovered his vocation. The onlooker, who has been learning how to hold a mirror up to those around him, will finally look inside himself and find treasures that are worth far more than anything outside himself. But for a long time he will seem to be adding one notation to another to complete the portraits he had already begun of characters about whom he had already kept us informed. No new person enters his life. That in itself should be enough to show us readers that he is growing old, although it will not be until the end of the book that he realizes this truth himself.

Saint-Loup pays flying visits to Tansonville, where we still find ourselves at the beginning of *Le Temps retrouvé*. Indeed, "flying" seems the appropriate word for Saint-Loup, whose visits to male brothels are characterized by the speed of his entrances and exits, a speed that affects all his movements. Another change in him is the hysterical, neurotic attitude that he now adopts with Gilberte, to whom he lies continually. Something of Morel seems to have rubbed off on him. Not that he fails to love Gilberte, at least in his own fashion. Just as Morel reminds him of Rachel, so too does Gilberte. In fact Gilberte tries to look like Rachel, to the point of painting her face and dying her hair. At the same time, while she apparently believes that her husband is having affairs with other women, she likes to gossip about homosexuals. In the course of conversation, the narrator questions her about Albertine, but quite mechanically and to no effect. They discuss *La Fille aux yeux d'or* (*The Girl with the Golden Eyes*) by Balzac, and the narrator reveals something of his life with

Albertine. Gilberte cannot believe that the narrator could have acted in such a manner. Again Proust reminds us about how we can be mistaken about the people we think we know. The narrator loses himself in hypotheses about Gilberte and Albertine.

The subject changes suddenly when the narrator reads a passage of the Goncourt *Journal* that describes a dinner party with the Verdurins. This pastiche, which includes some surprising information about M. and Mme Verdurin and their claims to be in the vanguard of the arts, disappoints the narrator and makes him wonder if literature is something factitious, since it makes the Verdurins seem interesting. At any rate, he has to recognize that he would be incapable of looking and listening in the manner of the Goncourts, because he does not look at people: he X-rays them. But he has to recognize that it is the artist who enhances the model, not the other way around.

Then he has to give up these reflections and go into a sanatorium, from which, apart from one trip to Paris in 1914 for a medical exam, he does not emerge until early 1916, in the midst of wartime Paris. He finds himself in a city of women wearing fashions that are so many allusions to the war, when they are not actually wearing jewelry made by the soldiers. Proust compares this Paris to that of the Directory, furbished by Napoleon's Egyptian campaign, and Mme Verdurin and Mme Bontemps are its queens. The narrator is quite amused by the frivolity and social climbing of these wartime women. He also comments that the people who had been excluded from the government and the highest levels of society for supporting Dreyfus during the Dreyfus affair are now running the government and leading society. What is necessary today is hatred of Germany and the determination to trample the Germans in the dust. Mme Verdurin is in a position to give advance information to her friends on official decisions and policy, so that she has many more friends than she used to have and has lost her inverted snobbery.

She can still offer Morel to her friends, in between discussing the war, because Morel is a deserter, although nobody knows this. Somebody else who is still around is Andrée's husband, although Andrée is a better friend than he is. Odette also comes to the fore, although Mme Verdurin does not succeed in taking up with her again—for the time being, at any rate.

When the narrator returned to Paris in 1914, he saw M. de Charlus, Bloch, and Saint-Loup. Saint-Loup seemed to have got over the hysterical insincerity that had afflicted him during the narrator's visit to Tansonville. Saint-Loup said that the men who were not at the front, as he was not, were cowards, while Bloch expressed the most ardent patriotism. But the facts eventually show the narrator that Saint-Loup was speaking out of modesty, and had been pulling strings to get himself accepted for military service, while the real coward was Bloch. (Saint-Loup had resigned his commission on marrying Gilberte, so he was no longer a regular officer.) That does not stop Bloch from insulting Saint-Loup, without annoying the latter in the slightest, for referring politely to the kaiser. Saint-Loup's homosexuality counts for something in his desire to fight, because he believes in an ideal of virility similar to that expressed by his uncle.

Staying only long enough in Paris to record the ways the butler torments Françoise with his version of the war news, the narrator had gone back to his sanatorium. Although the patients in the sanatorium are kept in isolation, he receives a letter from Gilberte, telling how she had taken refuge in Tansonville, only to find herself in the center of operations and obliged to open her house to the Germans, and a letter from Robert, full of ardent military comments, but without the slightest sign of personal animosity against the Germans as a nation.

Back in Paris in 1916, the narrator gets another letter from Gilberte in which she claims not to have fled for refuge to Tansonville but to have gone there to defend it from the German occupation. This is the official version, for there is a possibility that she will be decorated for bravery. She gives him news of the ravages of war around Combray. Then Saint-Loup comes to see him. The narrator is deeply moved by this spectacle of a soldier on leave, back from the front, as if risen from the dead. They talk of an air raid, and Saint-Loup insists on the aesthetic side of aerial combats; he compares the sirens to the music of Wagner and in particular to "The Ride of the Valkyries." The narrator, carried away by this comparison, goes on to speak of the Parisians who could be seen in the street in their nightwear. Then they talk strategy—or, rather, Saint-Loup does.

The narrator remembers this conversation as he wanders through wartime Paris and loses himself in the semiblackout. He gets onto the boulevards, which are full of Allied soldiers in the most varied uniforms, and runs into M. de Charlus, whom he identifies as a homosexual before recognizing him as an individual. The Baron's appearance is against him, as well as the absurd calumnies of Mme Verdurin, who denounces him as a Prussian spy. Not that the narrator pays the slightest attention to what Mme Verdurin has to say. But he recognizes that the Baron is isolated, even if the real reason is his penchant for quarreling with his family and friends, together with his old-fashioned taste for prewar elegance. Morel, whom the Baron had encouraged to publish, is launching vicious attacks on his former protector in the newspapers, satirizing his homosexuality and his pro-German feelings at the same time. But the chief effect of the wartime atmosphere on the Baron is to make him turn from adults to little boys, or so the narrator says, although he supplies little evidence for this conclusion.

Cottard and M. Verdurin die (for good, this time) and Elstir mourns M. Verdurin, who had had the most accurate vision of his art. But the narrator has very little to say about this subject. Mme Verdurin continues to give dinner parties and M. de Charlus goes in search of his pleasures, without interrupting these activities for bereavement or the war, even though the Germans are within an hour of Paris. Obviously they are aware that the war is going on, and Charlus even turns his house into a hospital for wounded soldiers, but their personal pleasures are more important than national concerns. For instance, Mme Verdurin dunks her croissant in her coffee with great satisfaction while reading of the sinking of the *Lusitania*.

M. de Charlus is less devoted to the war effort than Mme Verdurin, for he does not want the Germans to be crushed. Because his mother was a Bavarian duchess, he is not really French. Moreover, he is irritated by the stupidity of many patriots, he feels sorry for Germany because he is sure that it will not win the war, he resents men of honor who find it easy to condemn a rascal, and his form of homosexuality makes him see the English, who strike him as handsome, as the pitiless executioners of the Germans, whom he considers ugly but virtuous. The English dominance of the Germans might appeal to his sadomasochism, but cannot appeal to his compassionate side.

M. de Charlus chats to the narrator, as they walk along the boulevards, abut the war articles written by Brichot and Norpois, in a very entertaining way, and goes on to comment on European politics in a manner that owes more to his cult of nobility and to his homosexuality than to his intelligence. At this point, the narrator interrupts his account of Charlus's conversation to tell us that Brichot's articles, which had aroused enthusiasm in the Faubourg Saint-Germain, are mocked by Mme Verdurin, with considerable success. Then we are back with Charlus, who is regretting the death of so many handsome young men, which he considers as much of a loss, from the point of view of art, as the destruction of Rheims cathedral. He goes on to speak of the destruction of the church of Combray, and he and the narrator argue a little about whether Saint Firmin's raised arm, at Amiens, is broken, and whether that means that the highest symbol of faith and energy has disappeared from the world. Both agree in the end that people are more important than the stones that represent them.

M. de Charlus continues to talk about the war at the top of his voice; when he starts saying that Germany is strong, the narrator begs him to moderate his tone. M. de Charlus is simply amused at the idea of having shocked the passersby by sounding like a defeatist. He says that if he were shot in the ditches of Vincennes, it would be no more than what had happened to his great-uncle the Duc d'Enghien, for the populace is always avid for noble blood. As he talks, some very suspicious-looking characters move out of the shadows and follow him at a distance, so that the narrator wonders whether the Baron would prefer to be left in their company or protected from it. But it seems that the Baron would prefer to avoid them, for he draws the narrator into a side street full of soldiers. Indeed, there are soldiers even in the sky, for the airplanes are rising and the searchlights are scanning the sky. The Baron de Charlus expresses his admiration for aviators, no less the German ones than the French.

Then he switches his topic to Mme Verdurin and Morel, and suggests that the narrator might let Morel know that the Baron would be glad to see him. In fact, the narrator runs into Morel two or three years later and insists that he really should go and see the Baron. Morel absolutely refuses to go, and finally admits that he is afraid to go near the Baron. Morel's fear turns out to be justified when, after the Baron's death, the narrator is given a letter from the latter, written 10 years earlier, in which he says that he had made up his mind to murder Morel if the latter came to see him, and that Morel had been directly inspired by God to stay away.

Getting back to their walk along the boulevards, the Baron proceeds to talk about what would be preserved of Paris, as a modern Pompeii with the inscription *Sodoma*, if it were buried under a German volcanic explosion. Then he goes on to express his admiration for the English and French soldiers, but also for the Germans. Shortly afterward, the Baron says he has decided to go home, where he will still be surrounded by soldiers. But before he leaves, he pauses to admire a Senegalese soldier and to speak of the incursion of the Orient, with all its picturesqueness, into Paris.

Left alone in a labyrinth of side streets, the narrator muses on the *Arabian Nights* and feels like Haroun al Rashid exploring his city by night. He will refer again to the *Arabian Nights* at the end of this volume, to say that the book he intends to write will be like the *Arabian Nights*, even though he has no intention of copying it. The narrator's curiosity, so easily aroused; the transformations his characters undergo, even the suggestion that the Guermantes are descended from the union of a goddess and a bird; the narrator's amazement at the astonishing adventures that befall him; the secrets that various houses conceal—all combine to give the same impression as the *Arabian Nights*. And now the narrator's most astonishing adventure is about to take place, although all he is looking for is a place to rest a little and have something to drink before making his way back to his apartment.

The district he is in seems characterized by poverty, abandonment, and fear, for everything is closed—everything except one building with lighted windows and customers going in and out. He even thinks he sees Saint-Loup coming out, but the officer disappears immediately without seeing him. The narrator wonders, because Saint-Loup has been accused of espionage at one point, whether this building is a meeting place for spies. He decides to go in to satisfy, at one and the same time, his thirst and his curiosity. He enters, and sees that some customers are favored with rooms and others not. Some soldiers and working men are chatting in a little room where he can watch them without being seen himself. They are expressing patriotic ideas, which do not sort very well with his hypothesis that they are spies. The narrator, disappointed by the normality of this conversation, is about to leave when he is horrified to overhear some remarks about getting chains to tie up someone who is already tied up but not securely enough. Obviously a dreadful crime is about to be committed. Imagining that he is in a dream or a fantastic tale, the narrator steps right into the hotel, feeling both like a poet and a minister of justice.

In order not to arouse the suspicions of the assassins, he asks for a room and something to drink. But he is told to wait for the manager to come back. The young men make room for him, and continue their conversation about the war and their comrades, particularly one called "le grand Julot," whom they despise for not being a pimp, even though he calls himself one, but of whom they have a good opinion otherwise. After that, a chauffeur with a magnificent watch chain comes in, and he gets a look of congratulation for having stolen it. Obviously these young men are not particularly moral. Then the manager comes back, carrying chains, lets the narrator have a room, and sends the young men off on various errands.

The narrator is soon escorted to his room, but he does not like the atmosphere, and goes wandering around to a room from which he thinks he hears muffled cries. Putting his ear to the door, he hears someone begging to be beaten more gently and someone else replying in rough, merciless tones. Then comes the sound of a lash, followed by cries of pain. The narrator finds a spy window in the wall and peeps in, to be rewarded by the sight of M. de Charlus, chained to a bed and covered with wounds, while Maurice, one of the young men from downstairs, lashes him with a cat o'nine tails. Just then the door opens and Jupien comes in. M. de Charlus sends the young man out for a moment, and complains to Jupien that his torturer is not brutal enough and does not insult him with sufficient conviction. Jupien reassures the Baron by saying that Maurice had been implicated in the murder of a concierge. Then he goes on to suggest that the Baron might like to try the man from the slaughter-house, and the Baron agrees. The narrator notices that both these young men bear a certain resemblance to Morel.

He then descends to the little antechamber, where the young men are praising an officer who had died in the defense of his orderly. They are deeply moved, particularly Maurice, whose only reason for embarking on this career is that he does not like ordinary work. These male prostitutes have courage and good hearts, as M. de Charlus had suspected, and believe that they have to kill the Germans because they are barbarians. At the same time, they take pride in their work, and Maurice does not want to admit that he has not given satisfaction.

While waiting to pay the manager, the narrator observes the comings and goings in a way that suggests that he understands what is going on and has a complete sympathy with it. His position is rather anomalous, since he is not an ordinary customer, and yet no one seems to question his presence or even ask if he would like to avail himself of the facilities. He seems as privileged a visitor to this homosexual brothel as to the Duc and Duchesse de Guermantes. Perhaps the inmates recognize him as a voyeur. (There is a very comical article on this episode by Jean Ferry which claims that the whole account is so fantastic as to amount to science fiction.)[1] Then Jupien comes in, is astonished to see the narrator, and starts to send the young men away. But the narrator says that it would be easier to talk outside. However, even outside he continues to hear requests for a domestic servant, a choirboy, or a black chauffeur. Other customers want Canadians, Scotsmen, or even an amputee. Then, apparently, the two are back in the hotel again, because the Baron is coming downstairs, and Jupien hides the narrator in a room that has just been vacated by the Vicomte de Courvoisier and from which he can hear and see without being seen.

From this vantage point he espies the Baron, with all the graces of a great lady, saying goodnight to his harem in the most vulgar argot. The Baron seems to be delighted by the crimes Jupien claims they have committed. In fact their immorality does not go very deep, and the Baron is quite mistaken in thinking that one of them would admit to accepting money from women or that Maurice would actually boast of having helped to murder a concierge. In fact, Maurice denies this murder categorically, which has the effect of pouring cold water on the Baron's enthusiasm. What is even more disappointing for the Baron is that Maurice says he will send some of the money he has just earned to his parents and some to his brother, who is at the front. The young men utter confessions they hope will sound perverse, but these attempts only disappoint the Baron even more.

We learn that the Prince de Foix also used to frequent this brothel, although the Baron has never seen him there, and that one of the most assiduous customers is a bad priest. Then a young man arrives who objects to the narrator's presence. He is the first to see anything unusual in it. At this point Jupien accompanies the narrator into the street. He tells the narrator that he keeps this house in order to provide the Baron with entertainment in his old age. By this he means not only the sexual entertainment the Baron receives, but also the enjoyment he gets from associating with these young men. The narrator thinks it is a pity that the Baron is not a novelist or a poet, because his life is full of distress that a writer could have turned to advantage. But the Baron is only a dilettante, not a writer.

Jupien goes on to defend himself for earning his living in this way, and argues that everyone is willing to earn money for doing things he likes. Without contradicting him, the narrator says that like the caliph of the *Arabian Nights* he had thought he was coming to the aid of someone who was being beaten, and then he had found himself in another story, one where a woman in the shape of a dog submitted voluntarily to being beaten in order to regain her original shape. Jupien is disturbed at this indication that the narrator had seen the Baron being beaten, but proceeds to joke about the narrator's (and Proust's) translation of Ruskin's *Sesame and Lilies*. His sesame is the light in his window, he says, but he has no lilies.

Just then a violent air raid begins, and the narrator loses his way, only finding it again by the light of a house on fire. He wonders if Jupien's hotel has received a hit and thinks of what the Baron had said about Paris and Pompeii. There is something grotesque about these people who go in search of their pleasures while under the threat of death. Not only in Jupien's hotel, but also in the darkened metro used as an air-raid shelter, people fall into each other's arms in a blind sexual frenzy. They no longer have to fear the police, since the police are more interested in safeguarding their lives than in judging their morals.

The narrator meditates on the scenes in Jupien's hotel as he goes home. He comes to the conclusion that there is a certain element of fetishism in the most normal loves, and even if this fetishism seems to have eliminated everything else in activities such as those of M. de Charlus, there is still a poetic element in those activities that can be traced back to the Baron's cult of virility. This argument typifies the way in which Proust both seems to make homosexuals look as grotesque and comic as possible, to exonerate himself in the eyes of those readers who despise homosexuals, and then justifies and rehabilitates them. Prometheus chained to the rock of matter, which is the narrator's first impression of the Baron de Charlus on viewing the sadomasochistic scene, becomes the vision of a poet, on last analysis.

The all-clear sounds as the narrator reaches his apartment building. Françoise and the butler come up from the cellar and say that Saint-Loup had dropped in to see if he had left his Croix de Guerre (French Medal of Honor) in the narrator's apartment. (In fact he had left it in Jupien's hotel.) He was looking for Morel at the same time, but without success. The two servants look for his medal, but without enthusiasm, because they consider the way Saint-Loup talks about the Germans unpatriotic.

The narrator had intended to leave Paris shortly, but he receives a piece of bad news that makes him too ill to travel. He learns that Saint-Loup has been killed in action while covering the retreat of his men. There follows a panegyric on Saint-Loup, in which he is praised for his impartiality toward the Germans and for his predilection for serving in danger zones. Full of a modesty that led him to prefer others to himself, he had not thought of his own safety, any more than in civilian life. The narrator remains shut up in his room for several days, thinking of Saint-Loup and remembering all the circumstances of their friendship. In spite of his recent visit to Jupien's hotel, the narrator cannot blame Saint-Loup for his homosexuality but instead remembers what a delightful, self-effacing friend he has been. He remembers Albertine at the same time, since she too died young and there were parallels between her life and Saint-Loup's, although he misses her far less. But he grieves over the fact that they both died so young, whereas he, who is so ill, is still alive. He remembers that Saint-Loup had a presentiment that he would die young and he wonders, very tenderly, if Saint-Loup's feelings of guilt over his homosexuality had anything to do with his presentiment.

Françoise mourns Saint-Loup too, but in a way that seems to the narrator like an infringement on his privacy, and the Duchesse de Guermantes actually mourns Saint-Loup for a week! She is also very kind to the exiled Russian archdukes and archduchesses, although she had been rude to the Russian royal family when she was young. These two facts make the narrator think that she has more heart than he had supposed. Meanwhile, Morel has been arrested as a deserter, as a result of the attempts Saint-Loup had made to trace him, and, thinking that he has been arrested because of M. de Charlus, he has M. de Charlus and M. d'Argencourt (a minor character who frequents homosexuals without being one himself) arrested in their turn. But they are shortly freed. Morel, when his general gets the news that Saint-Loup has died a hero's death, is sent to the front where he distinguishes himself and receives the Croix de Guerre whereas M. de Charlus had been unable to get the cross of the Legion of Honor for him.

The narrator notes that he has often thought since that Saint-Loup's medal would have enabled him to get elected after the war. But perhaps he would not have had the right kind of political rhetoric. People who were worth far less than he was had successful political careers.

There follows a gap in the narrative, during which the narrator spends several fruitless years in a sanatorium. Then the real "Time Regained" begins. I say the real Time Regained, because from now on the narrator will garner the involuntary memories that, like the madeleine episode, will give new meaning to his life and to his vocation as a writer, even though it does not look like that at first. In fact, what is chiefly on his mind as he sits in the Paris train is the thought of his lack of literary gifts, a thought that came to him during his walks with Gilberte at Tansonville, and to which his reading of the Goncourt *Journal* at Tansonville put a finishing touch by almost completely convincing him of the emptiness and mendacity of literature. He had not thought of his disillusionment in this respect for some time, but now it hits him with redoubled force.

The train has stopped in some open countryside, where the sun shines halfway down the trunks on a row of trees. He mentally addresses the trees, saying to them that he gets no pleasure whatever from seeing the sun on them, for his heart is cold and he can no longer believe that he is a poet. The years when he could celebrate nature have gone forever, although he may be able to study mankind. But he knows that this idea of studying mankind is only a consolation, and a valueless one at that. He is obviously in a state of deep depression, which he calls ennui and indifference. A state of indifference is the most painful sensation he can experience, because it means a lack of life. Even though he was no Christian, Proust here indicates that he wanted to have life and to have it more abundantly.

On returning to Paris, the narrator finds that his friends have not forgotten him, for he has received invitations from Berma and the Prince de Guermantes. He decides to accept the Guermantes invitation, because he has so many childhood associations with the name, which he has forgotten for so many years. The narrator takes a carriage to the Prince's new house, and he has a delicious feeling of smoothness and ease as they approach the Champs-Elysées because he is retracing the same path he used to take to the Champs-Elysées with Françoise when he was a boy. He is carried off into the realm of memory, where there are associations with Gilberte and Albertine as well as with his boyhood days.

When they reach the Champs-Elysées, he gets out, as he is not in a hurry to hear the concert at the Guermanteses', and sees another carriage stopping. It contains the Baron de Charlus, sitting in a state of semicollapse as the result of a recent stroke, with snow-white hair cascading from under his hat and from his chin. He seems to have the majesty of a King Lear. He had lost his sight for a while, but now he has recovered it, but he has permanently lost his aristocratic pride. When Mme de Sainte-Euverte passes by in a victoria and Jupien points her out to him, the Baron raises his hat to her with a humility that shows how little earthly greatness counts.

The Baron gets out of the carriage and chats with the narrator for a while in a whisper, only raising his voice when he enumerates all his friends who are dead. Then he sits down to study a book of prayers while Jupien and the narrator take a little walk. Jupien tells the narrator that, in spite of the Baron's illness and temporary blindness, he has to keep an eye on the Baron all the time because the Baron is constantly making new sexual conquests and he gives all his money away in the process. He has also taken to talking about his admiration for Germany and his homosexuality, regardless of who is listening.

After this chat, the narrator gets back into his carriage but gets out again near the home of the Princesse de Guermantes. He feels pleasure at the prospect of his visit, and he also feels that there is no further reason for him to deny himself these social pleasures, as his attempts to remember things that had given him pleasure, such as his trip to Venice, are simply depressing. He sees no particular advantage in living for a long time,

,since nothing really new can enter his life. But, now Proust tells us, it is sometimes at the moment when all seems lost that the signal comes that can save us. We have knocked on all the doors that open into nothing and we finally bump into the only one through which we can enter, without even knowing what we are doing, and for which we could have searched for a hundred years.

Getting out of the way of an approaching streetcar, at the warning cry of the driver, the narrator finds himself standing on two pavingstones of unequal height, and immediately his doubts about literature and his talent disappear. He is flooded by the same joy that had been incited earlier by the madeleine, the steeples of Martinville, the trees he had seen on a drive near Balbec, and the last works of Vinteuil. What this tactile sensation, similar to the one he had had in the baptistry of Saint Mark's, has brought to him is a true, involuntary memory of Venice, quite different from the insignificant snapshots of Venice that are all his voluntary memory can produce. But he still does not know why his memories of Combray and Venice should have brought him a joy like a certitude, sufficient, without any other proof, to make death seem unimportant to him.

He goes into the Guermantes residence, determined to find the answer to his question, and is asked to wait in the library next to the buffet for the piece of music that is being played to end. While he is waiting, a servant knocks a spoon against a plate, making a sound like that of a railroad employee tapping a wheel with a hammer, and he is immediately carried back to that moment when he had been sitting in the train gloomily contemplating the row of trees, but this time he relives that moment in joy. The signs that are to draw him out of his discouragement and give him renewed faith in literature are amazingly multiplied. When the butler brings him a plate of petits-fours and a glass of orangeade, the napkin with which he wipes his lips carries him back to Balbec, for it is as stiff and starched as the towel he had used there. He sees the waves, as he had seen the line of trees and the sunshine of Venice, as so real that he wonders for a moment if he is actually going to see the Princesse de Guermantes or if her residence is not going to collapse beneath him. He feels a joy far greater than he had actually felt at Balbec.

Waiting for the piece of music to end, the narrator quickly attempts to understand the nature of these pleasures he has experienced in the last few minutes. He realizes that there is no connection between voluntary and involuntary memory and that the whole ambience of a particular moment, discarded by the intelligence, remains enclosed in a spiritual

container of which there are many separate ones in our life. If by chance
we open one of these containers, we breathe in from it a purer air, the air
of paradise, because the real paradises are the ones we have lost. At last he
contains and is contained once more in a container. He feels ready to start
writing his book, but he recognizes that he cannot build it on involuntary memory alone. Then he goes on to reflect some more on these
moments of felicity. What they have in common is that they make him
exist simultaneously in the present and in the past, so that he is outside
of time. That was what made him so happy and so confident. They make
him exist in his essence, outside contingency. He had often been unhappy in the past because his imagination can only be applied to what is
absent and cannot find beauty in what is present. Now he can enjoy
something that is present and absent at the same time—a piece of time in
its pure state, in its essence.

While he is pondering this realization, a noise in a water pipe, which
sounds just like the siren of a steamer, takes him back to Balbec again and
he sees the hotel dining room, as clearly as he had seen Venice, the
countryside around the train, and the sea by the beach at Balbec. This
involuntary memory, like the others, is so real that the narrator says that
he would have lost consciousness if it had gone on any longer. These
involuntary memories are fugitive, but they are the most real part of the
narrator's existence because they rise up from within himself. Going
back to the places they evoke would be useless, but they might find their
equivalent in the music of Vinteuil. Another equivalent would be the
effort the narrator used to make, on looking at some object, to discover
the message it brought to him. This decoding effort is difficult, but it
reveals truths, and is the only way to arrive at truth, for it converts an
object or an experience into its spiritual equivalent. And what is that but
the creation of a work of art?

For a good many pages the narrator reflects on the nature of a work of
art and, in particular, on the nature of the book he intends to write. Even
though he says that putting theories in a book is like leaving the price
label on an object, this section of the book is full of literary theories.
What he disparages as putting theories in a book is, I think, any form of
authorial intervention that tells the reader what to think of the behavior
of the characters, instead of letting the facts speak for themselves. A
theory of this nature, I suggest, might include Jules Romains's unani-
mism or, looking ahead, Jean-Paul Sartre's existentialism. One might
also mention François Mauriac's Catholicism. It would be a case, Proust
goes on, of writing a book to fit a preconceived philosophy of life, instead

of drawing on life as it is lived, with all its surprises and contradictions, and accepting much that is mysterious in it. Proust's narrator often tells us what to think of the other characters' behavior, but he is frequently wrong. He comes close to being omniscient at times, but he is not omniscient. Intelligent and perceptive as he is, he is not superhuman. He simply has a special talent for the task of decoding what is not clear, of recognizing laws, of reacting positively to what is given to him and not to what he has deliberately sought out.

As Gilles Deleuze points out, he has to read the signs that are presented to him and that no one else can read for him, in an act of creation that most people avoid.[2] Excuses and good intentions do not count in art, which is what makes art so real, the most austere school of life and the true Last Judgment. The writer has to go by the actual impression things have made on him. For a moment these reflections are interrupted by a ray of sunshine that takes him back to Eulalie's room, and then he goes on to say that the work of art already exists and we have to discover it. But this act of discovery is actually the discovery of our real life. He dismisses current literary theories, particularly realism, which actually gives a false picture of life. Reasoning about what one writes means avoiding the real issue.

As he cogitates, he picks up one volume after another in the Prince de Guermanteses' library, and happens upon George Sand's *François le Champi.* This discovery brings him back to the *drame du coucher*, when his mother sat up all night reading *Françoise le Champi* to him. He has another involuntary memory. Though not a happy one, it is as rich in meaning and significance as the other involuntary memories are, since it carries him back into his past. The title and the color of the cover of this book are responsible for his memory. If he were a bibliophile like the Prince de Guermantes, the first editions he would collect would be the editions in which he read certain books for the first time or in particular places.

He goes on to say that he has no use for popular art, any more than for patriotic art. He believes that working-class people are not interested in reading about themselves. As for patriotic art, the artist serves the glory of his country best by simply painting as well as he knows how. Neither is it necessary to conform to an age of speed by writing short books or to the invention of the cinema by adopting a cinematographic technique. What is essential is the use of metaphor to bring together things that appear to be different, in order to underline the multiple connections of things. Thus the writer will translate the reality around him. This task of translation will also find its proper sphere when correcting what is said out of love or vanity and bringing it down to its proper dimensions. This same task of translation also applies to artistic impressions and any other impressions we share with others and for which we are tempted to have recourse to the lowest common denominator.

Many stay at this level, as celibates of art, unable to find any personal fecundity in the works of art they seek out so often. They are unable to assimilate what is truly nourishing in art. They suffer from an artistic bulimia, but they are nature's first attempts at artists. The attitude of those who merely appreciate art also leads to constant changes in artistic fashions, fashions that are often completely hollow. As for those who truly understand the work of a master, they are nothing but the full awareness of someone else. According to Proust, we all ought to be artists, for the artist lives on a far higher level than those who merely appreciate his art.

A writer who simply notes down the appearance of life is very far from reaching the reality of life. True life, life as it is discovered and illuminated, is literature. The same life dwells in all men, but they do not see it because they do not attempt to shed light on it. Style is a question of vision. It is the revelation of the qualitative difference in which the world appears to each of us, a difference that without art would remain the secret of each of us. It is only through art that we can get outside ourselves and see the way in which others see the universe. A Rembrandt or a Vermeer is a star that continues to send us its light after the star is dead and the artist dies. This art that seems so complicated, because it steers us away from the practical concerns that we wrongly call life, is the only living art. It is difficult, because it means going against the grain of our natural tendencies, particularly where love is concerned. But the sufferings of love are a source of inspiration. It also means going against habit, particularly against social habits, and seeking out obscurity and silence.

One can use the truths furnished by intelligence, but they do not come to us at such a profound level. Still, they do very well as a framework for the really deep truths of involuntary memory. The narrator feels within him a host of such truths, some of which come to him in suffering, some in very ordinary pleasures. The truths that come to us through suffering can cause us joy. He realizes that his past life is the stuff of the book he has to write, and this discovery explains why he had never been able to find a topic for the books he had intended to write. His life is his vocation. The writer should not take notes: when he comes to write, his memory will supply him with all kinds of expressions and gestures. He has his sketchbook to hand, without realizing it. Even if he failed to notice so many things that other people notice, he had noticed other particulars that are more useful to him, because they illustrate psychological laws. And his sensitivity can supply what he lacks in imagination.

The topic of sensitivity leads him to sorrow. He regrets having to use the dead Albertine and his dead grandmother for a work that will do them no good. He feels particularly guilty remembering his grandmother, and longs to die alone, in pain, abandoned by one and all, by way of expiation. There are many others he can think of who seem to have lived and died only for his advantage, not for their own. At the same time, he is profaning his loves by offering them to other people, who will think of different women. A book is a huge cemetery, he says. But because the writer's work makes the particular general, it is not exempt from a certain joy, even though love brings us endless sufferings, sufferings that are more educational than happiness and that teach us that we are placing in the object what is actually in the spirit. This truth applies to homosexual loves as much as heterosexual ones.

The narrator goes on to say that his book is an optical instrument that may not suit every pair of eyes. This remark is particularly meant to apply to his treatment of homosexuality. It may also be true of dreams and his interest in them, for they bring different times together so readily that he had thought at one moment that they were the means for regaining time. He comments on the way he has seen people change with time. He has also seen his country change with time. Getting back to dreams, he says that they had done most to convince him of the subjective nature of reality.

As he reflects on his past life, he comments that most of its substance comes from Swann, for without Swann he would never have gone to Balbec or met Mme de Villeparisis. If it were not for that, his life would have been completely different. At this point the butler comes to inform the narrator that the first piece of music has ended and he can join the other guests. On his way to the reception rooms, the narrator continues his reflections. First of all, he thinks that he does not have to avoid society to think creatively, as he had once supposed. Then he thinks of similar impressions of involuntary memory in Chateaubriand, Nerval, and Baudelaire, which seem to authorize him to use involuntary memory in his own writing.

As Jean-Yves Tadié says, Proust frustrates the critics by saying everything himself.[3] But the narrator receives a shock when he enters the reception room, because everyone in it seems to have made him- or

herself up to appear much older. This episode is what Proustians know as
the *Bal de têtes*, from the kind of "costume" ball in which everyone wears
a mask, head covering, or other devices to disguise their appearance,
while wearing ordinary clothes. This shock interrupts his train of
thought for a while. Instead of thinking right away, as an ordinary,
sensible, uncreative person might, "Oh, we have all got older while I was
in the sanatorium," the narrator wanders from the host and hostess to the
guests in a state of wonder, noting the various changes, as if he really were
in the *Arabian Nights* and some evil enchanter had changed everyone's
appearance overnight. (I should add that Proust does not mention the
Arabian Nights at this point, but rather fairy plays and the fairy tales of
Perrault.) It would be tedious to enumerate all the changes the narrator
notes in those around him; suffice it to say that Proust brings to his
description such an impression of amazement and misunderstanding
that this part of the text is one of the most fascinating in his great novel.

Not only the appearance but the whole character has changed in some
instances. At his point the narrator finally realizes that the changes he
sees are the work of Time, which Proust writes with a capital T. The
astonishing old people the narrator sees around him are dolls embodying
Time, Time that is not normally visible and that to become visible seeks
out bodies on which it shines its magic lantern. The effects of Time vary
considerably, for some people the narrator sees are much younger-
looking than others. But what really strikes the narrator more than
anything else is that Time has passed for him too, because people tell him
he is old. Bloch looks old too. The narrator is distressed to realize that,
just when he has received the inspiration he needs to write his book, he
may be too old to write it.

Some of the people around him are completely unrecognizable. He
does recognize, in spite of the changes Time has wrought in them, the
Prince de Guermantes, M. d'Argencourt (although greatly changed),
the Duc and Duchesse de Guermantes, Bloch, Gilberte, M. de Cambremer, Legrandin, the Prince d'Agrigente, Ski, Mme de Forcheville, Mme
Verdurin as the new Princesse de Guermantes, and Morel. But he is quite
indignant that he should look visibly old to others. However, he does
decide that the effects of time will have an important place in the book he
intends to write, not only from the point of view of his characters'
appearance but also from the point of view of the changes time brings
about in their lives. As he had intuited, being in society does not
interrupt the train of thought that he had begun in the library. So he
continues his observations. Some people have actually improved with

time. Others have adopted the characteristics of their parents or of other relatives. Others would seem young if they did not have difficulty walking, or have changed in some ways but not in others. Some even seemed to have become younger. Odette seems not to have changed at all.

The opinion other people have of us changes with time, an axiom exemplified by a respected government minister who had once been arrested for taking bribes. Proust draws the moral that whatever humiliation one endures, it will come to an end. Bloch too points this moral: he now calls himself Jacques du Rozier, has got himself accepted by society, and has managed to make himself look like an Englishman. He asks the narrator to present him to the Prince de Guermantes, which the narrator does easily, for the time when he was intimidated by the Prince de Guermantes is long behind him. Bloch also asks about the Princesse de Guermantes, and the narrator tells him that she is the ex-Madame Verdurin, who had married the Duc de Duras after the death of her first husband. Of all the extraordinary effects of time in this novel, this is the most extraordinary, for one would have thought at earlier points that such a marriage was impossible. Another seemingly impossible event is that Morel should be universally recognized as such a moral person that his testimony alone has sufficed to condemn two people in a recent trial.

Society itself has changed, for in this salon are people whom the narrator does not know and who would never have been received there formerly. The people who visit the Guermantes salon now are not particularly impressed by it. The narrator compares the Faubourg Saint-Germain to a senile dowager who replies with timid smiles to insolent servants who invade her salons, drink her orangeade, and introduce their mistresses to her. The old order only exists in the memory of certain people. The leaders of society, for the present group of people, are Mme de Forcheville, the Princesse de Guermantes, and Bloch, who has made a name for himself as a writer. The Duchesse de Guermantes has lost her social standing because she spends so much time with actresses. Swann's social position is completely forgotten. This is quite normal and happens all the time, because the people the narrator remembers seem quite distinct and yet have all come together, as in the Saint-Loup and Cambremer marriages. The same actors play many parts, and the same person has a different character and a different social position at different times.

Something else that changes is what we remember of the people we know. We forgive people with time too, although our pardon is in part an effect of forgetfulness or indifference. We treat people differently with the passage of time. What we remember of people is not what they remember of us, either, as the narrator's relationship with Albertine illustrates. The difficulty of making real contacts that the narrator had experienced in Combray is also true on the social level. The Guermanteses owed much of their prestige for him to his imagination, but they had become old friends for all that, and they had become valuable friends precisely because of his imagination. Another old friend, whom he has difficulty recognizing because he takes her for her mother, is Gilberte. They talk of Robert, whom Gilberte now venerates. They discuss his views on strategy.

Gilberte still remembers that her husband had loved Rachel more than he loved her, so it will be unpleasant for her to have to listen to Rachel give a poetry recital at this reception. But Gilberte does not mention this. Instead she invites the narrator to attend literary conversations she holds at her home. The narrator has no intention of accepting this invitation, for he intends to seek solitude for his work the following day, and discussing literature would not help him in the least. Nor does he intend to let people come and call on him when he is working, because his duty to his work is more important than the duty of being polite or even kind. He will do far more for the people who seek his company by writing for them than by doing anything else. However, he does ask Gilberte to introduce him to young girls, who will evoke in him the dreams and distresses of the past. But he says to himself that this is not such a good idea, because all the girls and women he has loved were surrounded by mystery, and these new girls would have no mystery.

The Duchesse de Guermantes is chatting affectionately with Rachel, who is her best friend. Perhaps the Duchesse really did prefer the company of intelligent people to that of socialites all along. But perhaps this friendship with Rachel showed that she had no real understanding of what intelligence consisted of. And perhaps she cultivated Rachel simply to annoy Gilberte. Rachel, for her part, probably sought out Mme de Guermantes because Mme de Guermantes had insulted her in the past and consequently held a great deal of prestige for her. But the time for Rachel to recite has come.

Meanwhile, at the other end of Paris, Berma is waiting for guests to come to her tea, which she is giving in honor of her daughter and son-in-law. They make her lead a terrible life, sending her out to act when she is extremely ill, forcing her to attend festivities that exhaust her, making her take morphine injections that nearly kill her, and conducting extensive and noisy repairs in the building next to hers so that she cannot sleep at night. She loves her daughter and fears her son-in-law, so that she puts up with all this. But her guests on this occasion desert her for the Princesse de Guermantes and Rachel. For her, Rachel is not an actress but a whore, and when she realizes that only one of her guests is coming, she eats the cakes prepared for her tea as if she were at her own funeral.

Back at the Princesse de Guermanteses', Rachel is giving her recitation. Her presentation is so emotional and exaggerated that her audience does not know whether to think it grotesque or magnificent. For the poetry of La Fontaine, which is what she is reciting, it certainly seems overdone. The Princesse de Guermantes, at any rate, applauds frenetically. The Duchesse de Guermantes backs her up. Bloch tramples on people's feet to congratulate Rachel. Only Mme de Saint-Loup holds out—not that this troubles Rachel, who is so sure of her success that she makes extremely unkind remarks about Berma. But the narrator is quite sure that Berma is and always was far above Rachel.

He gets into conversation with the Duchesse, who changes the subject of Rachel to the subject of the Duc's mistresses and the people, such as M. de Bréauté and Swann, whom she and the narrator had once known. To the narrator's surprise, she talks as if she had always known him and he had met Swann through her. They talk about her red dress and her red shoes, and it does not occur to her that the reason the narrator remembers these items is their association in his mind with her cruelty to Swann. But she does remember that the narrator went home that evening to meet a girl whom he was expecting after midnight. It is with this indifference, for the narrator is now indifferent to Albertine, the girl in question, that we remember the dead.

Then the Duchesse gets back to Rachel again, and shows once more how fallible memory is, for she has completely forgotten how she once despised and insulted Rachel for her performance of Maeterlinck at her house. On the contrary, what she now remembers is that she praised and appreciated Rachel and tried to make everyone else praise and appreciate her too. At this moment, the daughter and son-in-law of Berma arrive and ask to speak to Rachel. Rachel keeps them hanging around and sends a message back to say that she has finished her recitations. She lets them beg for the favor of shaking her hand, and finally lets them in, thus triumphing over Berma, whom she plans to humiliate with this story. In fact Berma will die of the shock. (Proust himself was kind, but his imagination was cruel.)

The narrator switches to the Duc de Guermantes, who is in love with

Mme de Forcheville and sequesters her as the narrator had sequestered Albertine. Still handsome, he is a splendid ruin, like his brother. All three of them, the Duc, the Duchesse, and the Baron, have lost their social position with advancing age. Odette still seems miraculously young, and has gone back to being the kept woman she always has been, which is the way she behaves with the narrator, telling him stories of her love affairs with the idea that he will put them in a book. In fact the narrator finds them very unsatisfactory, because of everything she leaves out.

The Duchesse leads the narrator around various reception rooms, talking about society. The narrator asks her if she thinks it was unpleasant for Gilberte to listen to Rachel. The Duchesse, in return, makes some very unpleasant remarks about Gilberte who, according to her, never loved her husband. Robert had joined the army during the First World War and had been glad to die because Gilberte had made him so unhappy. If Gilberte had loved Robert, she would have made a scene over being obliged to listen to Rachel, instead of taking it so calmly. This view of Gilberte is surprising, to say the least, but Gilberte surprises the narrator even more by offering to introduce him to her own daughter, in response to the request he had expressed earlier.

Mlle de Saint-Loup interests the narrator very much, for she represents the conjunctions of the two "Ways" of his childhood. She also represents Combray and Balbec. Swann, of Combray, had sent him to Balbec and Robert had put him in touch with the Guermanteses. Odette, who had fascinated him when he saw her with his Uncle Adolphe, is her grandmother. His Uncle Adolphe's servant was the father of Morel, whom Robert had loved and for whom he had made Gilberte unhappy. Swann had been the first to speak to him of the music of Vinteuil and Gilberte had been the first to speak to him of Albertine. It was a result of speaking to Albertine about Vinteuil that he had discovered that Mlle Vinteuil was her special friend and he had then begun this sequestered life with her. It was Robert who had gone to bring back Albertine. All his social life had been connected with Mlle de Saint-Loup's family too. Even the Verdurins were connected with it. Swann had loved the sister of Legrandin, who had known M. de Charlus, whose adopted daughter the young Cambremer had married. And Mme Verdurin, to close the circle of the narrator's memories, had married a Guermantes. The whole thing adds up, by the different places connected with these people, not only to a living compendium but to a psychology in space.

The idea of Time acts as a spur to the narrator, and he bursts into a paean of joy at the thought of the work that lies ahead of him. Someone who should write such a book, he says, would conduct it like an offensive, bear with it like a fatigue, accept it like a rule of life, build it like a church, submit to it like a diet, overcome it like an obstacle, conquer it like a friendship, nourish it like a child, and create it like a world. But he then goes on to say that he has a more modest idea of his book and of its readers, who would be invited to read in themselves. He would pin his book together like a dress or cook it like Françoise's *boeuf mode*. But only if enough time remains to him before his death, which he wishes to delay as long as possible, for he is no longer willing to throw his life away, as he had been on the evenings when he came back drunk from Rivebelle. He does not fear death in itself, but only the destruction of the book that he alone can write. He realizes that he has already died several times. Death will only be a new forgetting, as he has forgotten Albertine. We all die so that the grass may grow, the grass of fruitful works, on which future generations will come to picnic.

He realizes a little later, after the Guermantes reception is over, when he nearly falls three times going down a staircase, that he has very little strength left. After writing two letters that exhaust him, he resolves to devote what strength he has left exclusively to his book. At this point he does not know whether his book will be a church where the faithful will gather or a druid monument that no one visits. But he is determined to go on with it, even though what he is writing meets with incomprehension. People compliment him on using a microscope when he is using a telescope, on seeking out details when he is establishing general laws.

He lives with death, and does not know whether the master of his destiny will let him live to finish his book, like another Scheherezade. Time is with us as long as we live, with all our past memories, but death will obliterate them. We totter at the top of the dizzy summit of our past years, as if we were on stilts. If he lives to write his book, he will show men living in an enormous stretch of Time. And with that, "Time" is his last word.

Conclusion

So we leave the narrator on the word "Time." So much wasted time has turned out not to be truly wasted, now that the narrator has finally found his vocation. Sheer perseverance has kept him on his quest, even when he seemed far from it, as when he went into society or suffered torments because of his twisted notion of love. He has triumphed in the end because he has never for one moment faltered in his in-depth analysis of the emotions he felt within himself. Society was a snare for him because of its superficiality, and it had ruined Swann. But it did not ruin the narrator because he saw the hidden psychological truths beneath this superficiality. Swann had succumbed to the mediocrity of his marriage to Odette, but through all the torments of love the narrator has lived his emotions in their full intensity, stripping away layer after layer of consciousness as if he were stripping off his skin.

Kolb pointed out years ago that it is because the portraiture of the narrator is so imprecise that we find it easy to identify with him (40). We cannot see ourselves as others see us or as we see others. Many critics have since elaborated on Kolb's idea. I would add to Kolb's observation another, that we do not judge our own emotions while we are in the grip of them, but only some time later, when we have become different people. This is very characteristic of the narrator, who is lacking in self-knowledge for a very long time. In a sense, as Sartre observed, the narrator has no immediately recognizable character.[1] In another sense, when we add together the pieces of information he gives us, a character does begin to emerge, as if we were putting together a jigsaw puzzle.

He is more of a social climber than he is willing to admit, although the aristocracy disappoints him when he enters their charmed circle. He is heterosexual but attractive *to* homosexuals and attracted *by* lesbians. Moreover, he seems to prefer masturbation to any other form of sexual activity. He is also a voyeur and seems to be well on the way, at one point, to be a child molester. He is cruel and tyrannical in his love affairs, since he never expresses love directly or believes that it can be returned, so he automatically resorts to manipulation and lies.

This is not a very pretty picture. It is a little puzzling to hear some people say that *A la recherche du temps perdu* is based on a lie because Proust is saying "I" in speaking as a heterosexual. If he had written his great novel simply to disguise his own sexual orientation, he certainly could have done it in a more flattering way. Given the touchiness of Proust on the subject of his homosexuality, one can understand that he would not have wished to make an open and frank avowal, like Gide. But the very weaknesses of the narrator are an "Open, Sesame" to the topics Proust wishes to discuss. It takes someone like this to learn, by trial and error, what Proust wants to tell us. We accept his message because we are sharing in this process along with the narrator.

To give the narrator his due, he does have virtues as well as faults. He is highly intelligent, sensitive, artistic, very perceptive, a welcome guest, and capable of inspiring long and lasting friendships. He is fascinated by the people around him and really succeeds in understanding them, except when he is blinded by passion. He leads us through a succession of different milieux and succeeds in making us feel that we have grasped their essential nature. The narrator's voyage of discovery is also the reader's.

The reader can also discover himself or herself in the process. If we really reflect on what the narrator is revealing to us about himself, it may lead us to acknowledge that we are just as egotistical, just as fond of pointing out the flaws in other people while remaining unaware of our own, and just as anxious to be admired and flattered by the people we admire. In this sense, *A la recherche du temps perdu* is a very moral book. As I noted in the preface, it is a bildungsroman. As the narrator goes from error to error before finally learning the true goal of his existence, so his reader may receive from his example at least the wish for his own errors to lead to the same conclusion.

Proust uses the words "vice" and "virtue" in a way that modern writers and critics would eschew. But he is not using these words in the uncritical manner in which a Victorian would. He loved the good, the true, and the beautiful, but of his characters few are good, true, or beautiful. For the human failings that stem from a weakness of some kind, Proust had endless tolerance and sympathy, but he needed no tolerance where great creative works were concerned. That is why *A la recherche du temps perdu* leads to the vocation of a great writer. Few of us can emulate him in that way, but at least we all can have some vision of greater maturity and understanding, some dedication to a superior goal, and this may well be supported by the narrator's and by Proust's example.

The Paris of former days serves as a background to Proust's great novel, but this does not prevent us from feeling its immediacy. Proust's artistic ideals are not those of the first quarter of the twentieth century, but he does not seem old-fashioned. On the contrary, his insights seem amazingly modern. He seems as outside of time as his narrator in his moments of involuntary memory, and all because he had such a piercing insight into eternal human nature. It is because of this that we can learn from him, but what we may learn depends on the reader. I can only invite you to read him.

Notes and References

Preface

1. Lois Marie Jaeck, *Marcel Proust and the Text as Macrometaphor* (Toronto: University of Toronto Press, 1990).
2. Philip Kolb, "Proust's Protagonist as a 'Beacon,'" *L'Esprit Créateur* 5, no. 1 (Spring 1965): 38–47; hereafter cited in text.
3. Germaine Brée, *The World of Marcel Proust* (London: Chatto and Windus, 1967), 165. Brée's use of this term as applied to Proust's great novel is now generally accepted.

Chapter One: Proust's Life and Works

1. *Correspondance de Marcel Proust, Vol. 1: 1880–1895,* ed. Philip Kolb, (Paris: Plon, 1970), 121–25.
2. Milton Hindus, *A Reader's Guide to Marcel Proust* (New York: Noonday Press, 1926), 210.
3. *Correspondance de Marcel Proust, Vol. 9: 1909,* 163.
4. Antoine Compagnon, *Proust entre deux siècles* (Paris: Seuil, 1989), 9; hereafter cited in text.

Chapter Two: Du côté de chez Swann (Swann's Way)

1. Robert Vigneron, "Désintégration de Marcel Proust," *Annales Publiées par la Faculté des Lettres de Toulouse,* littératures 8, année 9, fasc. 1 (1960): 113–45.
2. Alain Robbe-Grillet, *Les Gommes* (Paris: Editions de Minuit, 1953).
3. Raymond T. Riva, "Marcel Proust: An Immodest Proposal," *Criticism* (Summer 1968): 217–24. Riva takes up the parallel in a different way, stressing normal bisexuality.
4. This and all subsequent translations in the text are my own.
5. Maurice Samuel, "The Concealments of Marcel," *Commentary,* 29 (January 1960): 8–22.
6. Luc Fraisse, *L'Oeuvre cathédrale: Proust et l'architecture médiévale* (Paris: José Corti, 1990).
7. William Butler Yeats, "The Choice," *The Collected Poems of W. B. Yeats* (New York: Macmillan, 1962), 242.
8. Thomas Mann, *Erzählungen* (Oldenburg, Germany: S. Fischer, 1958), 273.
9. E. M. Forster, *Abinger Harvest* (London: Edward Arnold, 1953), 117–

18; *Two Cheers for Democracy* (London: Edward Arnold, 1972), 219. I owe thanks to Stella Slade, a Forster specialists, for these two references.

10. In a dedication to Jacques Lacretelle, Proust explained that the "little phrase" is based on Saint-Saëns, Wagner, Franck, Schubert, and Fauré; see *Contre Sainte-Beuve, Pastiches et mélanges, ct Essais et articles,* ed. Pierre Clarac and Yves Sandré (Paris: Gallimard, 1971), 565.

Chapter Three: A l'ombre des jeunes filles en fleurs (Within a Budding Grove)

1. Marcel Muller, *Les Voix narratives dans "La Recherche du temps perdu"* (Geneva: Droz, 1983). This critic divides the narrative voice into several different personae or functions. I tend more to see these voices as representing different stages in the narrator's development.
2. *Contre Sainte-Beuve,* 221–222.
3. *A l'ombre des jeunes filles en fleurs,* ed. Danièle Gasiglia-Laster (Paris: Flammarion, 1987), 1:256.
4. Gérard Genette, *Figures III* (Paris: Seuil, 1972), 53–54.
5. André Gide, *Journal 1889–1939* (Paris: Gallimard, 1965), 694.

Chapter Four: Le Côté de Guermantes (The Guermantes Way)

1. *Le Côté de Guermantes,* 2 vols. ed. Elyane Dezon-Jones (Paris: Flammarion, 1987), 1:67.
2. Roger Shattuck, *Proust* (London: William Collins Sons, 1974), 73; hereafter cited in text.

Chapter Five: Sodome et Gomorrhe (Cities of the Plain)

1. Melvin Seiden, "Proust's Marcel and Saint-Loup: Inversion Reconsidered," *Contemporary Literature* 10, no. 2 (Spring 1969): 220–40; also in Barbara J. Bucknall, ed., *Critical Essays on Marcel Proust* (Boston; G. K. Hall, 1987), 92–108.
2. *Sodome et Gomorrhe,* 2 vols., ed. Emily Eells-Ogée (Paris: Flammarion, 1987), 1:126; hereafter cited in text as *Sodome.*
3. Howard Moss, *The Magic Lantern of Marcel Proust* (London: Faber and Faber, 1963), 52; hereafter cited in text.
4. Bishop Reginald Heber, "From Greenland's Icy Mountains," a hymn that states that in the most beautiful surroundings "only man is vile." To be found in many hymn books, including *The Book of Common Praise* (Toronto: Oxford University Press. [n.d.] 254.

Chapter Six: La Prisonnière (The Captive)

1. Jean-Jacques Rousseau, *Les Confessions,* 2 vols. (Paris: Librairie Générale Française, 1963), 1:492.
2. *La Prisonnière,* ed. Jean Milly (Paris: Flammarion, 1984), 204; hereafter cited in text.

3. M. André-Brunet informed me that this expression is First World War soldiers' slang. It can also be found in Jacques Porel, *Fils de Réjane, Sourenirs,* vol. 1 (Paris: Plon, 1951), 98, where the meaning is apparent.

Chapter Seven: La Fugitive (Albertine disparue) (The Fugitive)

1. Leo Bersani, *Marcel Proust: The Fictions of Life and Art* (New York: Oxford University Press, 1965), 185.
2. *Correspondance de Marcel Proust, Vol. 13: 1914,* 217–21.
3. J. E. Rivers, *Proust and the Art of Love: The Aesthetics of Sexuality in the Life, Times, and Art of Marcel Proust* (New York: Columbia University Press, 1980), 248–49.
4. *La Fugitive (Albertine disparue)*, ed. Jean Milly (Paris: Flammarion, 1986), 318.

Chapter Eight: Le Temps retrouvé (Time Regained)

1. Jean Ferry, "Proust et la science fiction," *Cahiers du collège de 'pataphysique*, 88, n.s., 22 shitty month 92 [8 June 1965]: 55–68. The year 92 seems to be counting from the birth of Alfred Jarry, in whose honor the "college" was founded.
2. Gilles Deleuze, *Marcel Proust et les signes* (Paris: Presses universitaires de France, 1964).
3. Jean-Yves Tadié, *Proust et le roman* (Paris: Gallimard, 1971), 417–18.

Conclusion

1. Jean-Paul Sartre, *L'Etre et le néant: Essai d'ontologie phénoménologique* (Paris: Gallimard, 1943), 416.

Selected Bibliography

In the secondary sources I have listed bibliographies that cover the field up to 1982. Of the overwhelming number of books and articles devoted to Proust and his works, I have listed a few books and articles that I have found particularly helpful.

PRIMARY WORKS

Novels, Short Stories, and Novellas

A la recherche du temps perdu. 11 vols. Paris: Gallimard, 1919–27.
A la recherche du tempo perdu. 3 vols. Edited by Pierre Clarac and André Ferré. Paris: Gallimard, Bibliothèque de la Pléiade, 1954.
A la recherche du temps perdu. 11 vols. Edited by Jean Milly. Paris: Flammarion, 1984–87.
A la recherche du temps perdu. 3 vols. Edited by Bernard Raffali. Paris: Robert Laffont, 1987.
A la recherche du temps perdu. 4 vols. Edited by Jean-Yves Tadié. Paris: Gallimard, Bibliothèque de la Pléiade, 1987–89.
Albertine disparue. Edited by Nathalie Mauriac and Etienne Wolff. Paris: Grasset, 1987. (First edition of the last manuscript revised by the author.)
L'Indifférent. Preface by Philip Kolb. Paris: Gallimard, 1978.
Jean Santeuil. 3 vols. Edited by Bernard de Fallois. Paris: Gallimard, 1952.
"Jean Santeuil" précédé de "Les Plaisirs et les jours." Edited by Pierre Clarac and Yves Sandré. Paris: Gallimard, Bibliothèque de la Pléiade, 1971.
Les Plaisirs et les jours. Paris: Calmann Lévy, 1896.

Translations

La Bible d'Amiens. Translation with annotations and preface of *The Bible of Amiens,* by John Ruskin. Paris: Mercure de France, 1904.
Sésame et les lys: des trésore des rois; des jardins des reines. Translation with annotations and preface of *Sesame and Lilies,* by John Ruskin. Paris: Mercure de France, 1906.

Essays, Pastiches, and Prefaces

Chroniques. Collected by Robert Proust and Gaston Gallimard. Paris: Gallimard, 1927.

"Contre Sainte-Beuve" suivi de "Noveaux mélanges." Edited by Bernard de Fallois. Paris: Gallimard, 1954.

"Contre Sainte-Beuve" précéde de "Pastiches et mélanges" et suivi de "Essais et articles." Edited by Pierre Clarac and Yves Sandré. Paris: Gallimard, Bibliothèque de la Pléiade, 1971.

Pastiches et mélanges. Paris: Gallimard, 1919.

Les Pastiches de Proust. Edited by Jean Milly. Paris: Armand Colin, 1970.

Preface to *Propose de peintre,* vol. 1: *De David à Degas,* by Jacques-Emile Blanche. Paris: Emile Paul, 1919.

Preface to *Tendres stocks,* by Paul Morand. Paris: Gallimard, 1921.

Previously Uncollected works and Manuscripts

Le Carnet de 1908. Edited by Philip Kolb. *Cahiers Marcel Proust,* n.s.8. Paris: Gallimard, 1976.

Matinée chez la princess de Guermantes: Cahiers de "Temps retrouvé." Edited by Henri Bonnet and Bernard Brun. Paris: Gallimard, 1982.

Poèmes. Edited by Claude Francis and Fernande Gontier. *Cahiers Marcel Proust,* n.s. 10. Paris: Gallimard, 1982.

Textes retrouvés. Edited by Philip Kolb. *Cahiers Marcel Proust,* n.s. 3. Paris: Gallimard, 1971.

Correspondence

There have been many collections of Proust's letters, but these have been superseded by:

Correspondance. 19 vols. Edited by Philip Kolb. Paris: Plon, 1970—.

English Translations of Proust

The most reliable translations are:

Jean Santeuil. Translated by Gerard Hopkins. London: Weidenfeld and Nicolson, 1955.

On Reading Ruskin: Prefaces to "La Bible d'Amiens" and "Sésame et les lys," with Selections from the Notes to the Translated Texts. Translated and edited by Jean Autret, William Burford and Phillip J. Wolfe. Introduction by Richard Macksey. New Haven: Yale University Press, 1987.

Pleasures and Regrets. Translated by Louise Varese. London: Collins, Grafton Books, 1988.

Remembrance of Things Past. 3 vols. Translated by C.K. Scott Moncrieff and Terence Kilmartin. New York: Random House, Vintage Books, 1981.

SECONDARY WORKS

Books on Marcel Proust

Albaret, Céleste. *Monsieur Proust: Souvenirs recueillis par Georges Belmont.* Paris: Robert Laffont, 1973. Informative and affectionate reminiscences by Proust's housekeeper.

Bersani, Jacques, ed. *Les Critiques de notre temps et Proust.* Paris: Garnier, 1971; Essays by respected French critics, ranging from Proust's first publisher's report to Gérard Genette.

Bersani, Leo. *Marcel Proust: The Fictions of Life and of Art.* New York: Oxford University Press, 1965. Bersani connects the fantasies of the narrator with the form of *A la recherche du temps perdu.* A perceptive study.

Bonnet, Henri. *Alphonse Darlu (1849–1921) maître de philosophie de Marcel Proust.* Paris: A.G. Nizet, 1961. Important for the youthful Proust's intellectual development.

———. *Les Amours et la sexualité de Marcel Proust.* Paris: A.G. Nizet, 1985. A study of Proust's sex life based on biographical research.

———. *Le Progrès spirituel dans "La recherche" de Marcel Proust.* 2d ed. Paris: A.G. Nizet, 1979. Useful for Proust's philosophy of life.

Brée, Germaine. *The World of Marcel Proust.* London: Chatto and Windus, 1967. An excellent introduction that provides much information on Proust's social background and personal development.

Bucknall, Barbara J., ed. *Critical Essays on Marcel Proust.* Boston: G.K. Hall, 1987. An attempt to provide a representative panorama of Proust criticism.

Cocking, J.M. *Proust.* London: Bowes and Bowes, Studies in Modern European Literature and Thought, 1965. A very condensed introduction. A good guide for the beginning reader.

Compagnon, Antoine. *Proust entre deux siècles.* Paris: Seuil: 1989. Explains how Proust bridges the nineteenth and twentieth centuries. Draws on much previously unavailable material. Excellent for the advanced reader.

Deleuze, Gilles. *Proust et les signes.* Paris: Presses Universitaires de France, 1971. An account of *A la recherche de temps perdu* as a guide to a writer's apprenticeship. Semiotic without jargon.

Fraisse, Luc. *L'Oeuvre cathédrale.* Paris: José Corti, 1990. A dictionary guide to the connection between Proust's work and ecclesiastical architecture. Lengthy and informative.

Genette, Gérard and Tzvetan Todorov, eds. *Recherche de Proust.* Paris: Seuil: 1980. Essays by respected French critics from Gérard Genette to Philippe Lejeune.

Graham, Victor E. *The Imagery of Proust.* Oxford: Basil Blackwell, 1966. A detailed discussion of Proust's images. Unfortunately, all the references are to the first edition of *A la recherche du temps perdu.*

Green, F.C. *The Mind of Proust: A Detailed Interpretation of "A la recherche du temps perdu."* Cambridge: Cambridge University Press, 1949. A good introduction, much longer and more detailed than most.

Hayman, Ronald. *Proust: A Biography.* New York: HarperCollins, 1990. A more substantial biography than Painter's, using previously unavailable material. Unfortunately, the translations are not always accurate.

Mauriac, Claude. *Proust par lui-même.* Paris: Seuil, 1959. Brief but highly concentrated study of Proust's life and works.

Mein, Margaret. *A Foretaste of Proust: A Study of Proust and His Precursors.* Westmead, England: Saxon House/D.C. Heath, 1974. Discusses Proust's affinities with Pascal, Chateaubriand, Nerval, Baudelaire, Novalis, Balzac, George Eliot, Fromentin, and Flaubert.

Miller, Milton L. *Nostalgia: A Psychoanalytic Study of Marcel Proust.* London: Victor Gollancz, 1957. A psychoanalytic study of Proust. Seems convincing, but errs on the gloomy side. Does not explain Proust's greatness.

Milly, Jean. *Proust dans le texte et l'avant-texte.* Paris: Flammarion, 1985. Explains the benefits to be derived from studying Proust's variants. For the advanced reader.

Monnin-Hornung, Juliette. *Proust et la peinture.* Geneva: Droz: Lille, France: Giard, 1951. A ground-breaking study of the role of painting in *A la recherche du temps perdu.*

Moss, Howard. *The Magic Lantern of Marcel Proust.* London: Faber and Faber, 1963. Chiefly about the grandeur of Proust's projections and how they make his account seem magical.

Mouton, Jean. *Proust.* Bruges, Belgium: Desclée de Brouwer, Les Ecrivains devant Dieu, 1968. An assessment of Proust's religious beliefs or lack of them.

Muller, Marcel, *Les Voix narratives dans "La recherche du temps perdu."* Geneva: Droz, 1983. Identifies four different voices in *A la recherche du temps perdu,* namely the Hero, the Narrator, the Writer, and the Novelist.

Painter, George D. *Marcel Proust: A biography.* 2d ed. London: Chatto and Windus, 1989. The standard biography, but tends to confuse fact and fiction. Good for the originals of Proust's characters.

Picon, Gaëtan. *Lecture de Proust.* Paris: Mercure de France, 1963. A subtle and advanced reading. Has much to say about Proustian metaphor.

Price, Larkin B., ed. *Marcel Proust: A Critical Panorama.* Urbana: University of Illinois Press, 1973. A collection of essays by respected critics, mainly American.

Richard, Jean-Pierre. *Proust et le monde sensible.* Paris: Seuil, 1974. A study of desire and sensuality in Proust. Psychoanalytic and semiotic. For the advanced reader.

Rivers, Julius Edwin. *Proust and the Art of Love: The Aesthetics of Sexuality in the Life, Times, and Art of Marcel Proust.* New York: Columbia University Press,

1980. A serious and erudite exploration of the subject, with much historic detail.

Shattuck, Roger. *Proust*. London: Fontana/Collins, 1974. An introduction. Concentrates on the comic side of Proust.

———. *Proust's Binoculars: A Study of Memory, Time, and Recognition in "A la recherche du temps perdu."* New York: Random House, 1963. Concentrates on the way the Proustian vision is literally a way of seeing.

Tadié, Jean-Yves, ed. *Lectures de Proust*. Paris: Armand Colin, 1971. An overview of Proust's numerous critics from 1896 to 1970.

———. *Proust et le roman: Essai sur les formes et techniques du roman dans "A la recherche du temps perdu."* Paris: Gallimard, 1971. A serious and profound study. Recommended for the advanced reader.

Articles and Parts of Books on Proust

Ferry, Jean. "Proust et la science fiction." *Cahiers du collège de 'pataphysique* 88, n.s., 22 shitty month 92 (8 June 1965): 55–68. A send-up of the narrator's claim to objectivity.

Genette, Gérard. "Métonymie chez Proust." In *Figures III*. Paris: Seuil, 1972. A seminal discussion of metonymy and metaphor. For the advanced reader.

Johnson, J. Theodore, Jr. "From Artistic Celibacy to Artistic Contemplation." *Yale French Studies* 34 (1965): 81–89. A well-informed study of the importance of painting for Proust.

———. "'La Lanterne magique': Proust's Metaphorical Toy." *L'Esprit Créateur* 11, no. 1 (Spring 1971): 17–31. A study in projections.

Kolb, Philip. "Proust's Protagonist as a 'Beacon.'" *L'Esprit Créateur* 5, no. 1 (Spring 1965): 38–47. The creative triumph of the narrator and the way we identify with him. A seminal article.

Lejeune, Philippe. "Ecriture et sexualité." *Europe*, no. 502–3 (February–March 1971): 113–43. A Freudian interpretation. Very well known as part of a new departure in French Proust criticism.

Riva, Raymond T. "Marcel Proust: An Immodest Proposal." *Criticism* 10, no. 3 (Summer 1968): 217–24. Suggests that Proust can teach the reader about his own bisexuality.

Samuel, Maurice. "The Concealments of Marcel: Proust's Jewishness." *Commentary* 29 (January 1960): 8–22. Suggests that the narrator is a secret Jew.

Seiden, Melvin. "Proust's Marcel and Saint-Loup: Inversion Reconsidered." *Contemporary Literature* 10, no.2 (Spring 1969): 220–40. Also in Bucknall, Barbara J., ed., *Critical Essays on Proust*. Suggests that the narrator is secretly homosexual.

Vigneron, Robert. Désintégration de Marcel Proust." *Annales publiées par la Faculté des Lettres de Toulouse*, Literature 8, year 9, no.1 (1970): 113–45.

Series and Journals Devoted to Marcel Proust

Bulletin de la Sociefté des Amis de Marcel Proust et des Amis de Combray. 1950– .
Cahiers Marcel Proust, n.s. Paris: Gallimard, 1973–87.
Bulletin d'informations proustiennes. Paris: Ecole Normale Supérieure, 1975– .

Bibliographies on Marcel Proust

Alden, Douglas W. "Bibliography." In *Marcel Proust and His French Critics,*
171–259. New York: Russel and Russel, 1973. Covers Proust's critics in
detail from 1895 to 1939.
Bonnet, Henri. *Marcel Proust de 1907 à 1914.* 2 vols. 2d ed. Paris: Nizet,
1971–76. Provides extensive bibliography but does not always provide full
bibliographical details.
Brooks, Richard A., general ed., "Marcel Proust." In *A Critical Bibliography of
French Literature, Vol. 6: The Twentieth Century.* Edited by Douglas W.
Alden and Richard A. Brooks, part 1: 198–350. Syracuse, N.Y.: Syracuse
University Press, 1980. A meticulously annotated bibliography, indis-
pensable as a research tool.
Kolb, Philip, ed. "Les Publications de Marcel Proust: Bibliographie." In *Textes
retrouvés,* 377–408. A meticulous list of Proust's publications, down to
individual letters as they are discovered.
Rancoeur, René. "Bibliographie de Marcel Proust (1972 et compléments
1971)." In *Cahiers Marcel Proust*, n.s. 7, *Etudes proustiennes* 2, 283–95. Paris:
Gallimard, 1975.
———. "Bibliographie de Marcel Proust (1973 et 1974)." In *Cahiers Marcel
Proust*, n.s. 9, *Etudes proustiennes* 3, 349–68. Paris: Gallimard, 1979.
———. "Bibliographie de Marcel Proust (1975, 1976, et 1977)." In *Cahiers
Marcel Proust*, n.s. 11, *Etudes proustiennes 4: Proust et la critique anglo-saxonne,*
317–91. Paris: Gallimard, 1982.
———. "Bibliographie de Marcel Proust (1978, 1979, 1980, 1981)." In
Cahiers Marcel Proust, n.s. 12, *Etudes proustiennes* 5, 305–32. Paris: Galli-
mard, 1984.
———. "Bibliographie de Marcel Proust (1982 et compléments)." In *Cahiers
Marcel Proust,* n.s. 14. *Etudes proustiennes* 6, 339–49. Paris: Gallimard,
1987. No annotations, but brings Proustian bibliography up to date.

Index

The Author

Barbara J. Bucknall is associate professor of French literature at Brock University, Ontario, Canada. She received her B.A. degree from Oxford University and her Ph.D. from Northwestern University. She has published two other books on Proust, *The Religion of Art in Proust* (University of Illinois Press, 1969) and *Critical Essays on Marcel Proust* (G.K. Hall, 1987), an anthology of Proust criticism that she edited. She has also published several articles. Her other interests include fantasy, science fiction, children's books, and women's studies.

"If to be a Proustian is to be interested in nothing but Proust, then I am not one. I am interested in a great many branches of literature, not only in French. But if to be a Proustian is to fall in love with Proust, to be annoyed with him, to drop him for a while and then come back to him, seeing greater truth and greater complexity, then I am a Proustian."